MW00533123

Max
The Dog That Refused to Die
and
Pepper's Ordeal

Also by Kyra Petrovskaya Wayne

Kyra—Prentice-Hall, 1959
Kyra's Secrets of Russian Cooking—Prentice-Hall, 1960
The Quest for the Golden Fleece—Lothrop, Lee & Shepard, 1960
Shurik—Grosset and Dunlap, 1970
The Awakening—Grosset and Dunlap, 1973
The Witches of Barguzin—Thomas Nelson, 1975
Rekindle the Dreams—Dale, 1977
Max, the Dog That Refused to Die—Alpine, 1979
Quest for Empire—Hancock House, 1986
Li'l Ol' Charlie—Alpine, 1989
Quest for Bigfoot—Hancock House, 1996

Max
The Dog That Refused to Die
and
Pepper's Ordeal

by Kyra Petrovskaya Wayne

with illustrations by Becky Bristow
and Gordon Clover

hancock
house

ISBN 0-88839-477-2 (softcover)
ISBN 0-88839-476-4 (hardcover)
Copyright © 2000 Kyra Petrovskaya Wayne

Cataloging in Publication Data
Wayne, Kyra Petrovskaya.
Max : the dog that refused to die ; and, Pepper's ordeal

ISBN 0-88839-476-4 (bound) — ISBN 0-88839-477-2 (pbk.)

1. Dogs—Biography. 2. Dogs—Anecdotes. I. Title II. Title:
Pepper's ordeal.
SF426.2.W39 2000   818'.5403   C00-910152-7

All rights reserved. No part of this publication may be reproduced,
stored in a retrieval system or transmitted, in any form or by any means,
electronic, mechanical, photocopying, recording, or otherwise, without
the prior written permission of Hancock House Publishers.
Printed in Canada—Kromar

The first part of the present work, pp. 1–70, was originally published as *Max: The Dog That Refused
to Die* by Alpine Publications—recipient of the 1981 first prize award by the Dog Writers
Association of America. © 1979 Kyra Petrovskaya Wayne

Some names and locations in the present work have been fictionalized to protect the privacy
of certain individuals.

Editor: Nancy Miller
Production: Ingrid Luters
Front cover illustration: Becky Bristow

Published simultaneously in Canada and the United States by

HANCOCK HOUSE PUBLISHERS LTD.
19313 Zero Avenue, Surrey, B.C. V4P 1M7

HANCOCK HOUSE PUBLISHERS
1431 Harrison Avenue, Blaine, WA 98230-5005

(604) 538-1114   Fax (604) 538-2262
(800) 938-1114   Fax (800) 983-2262
Web Site: www.hancockhouse.com   *email:* sales@hancockhouse.com

Max: The Dog That Refused to Die

1981 First Prize Winner—Dog Writers Association of America

Dedicated to:
Sue Harrison,
Jo from Minnesota,
Dr. Richard H. Merrill and his staff
at Porterville Small Animal Hospital,
the doctors and staff of the West Los Angeles
Veterinary Medical Group,
the officers of the California Highway Patrol,
Don Lynn Matthews, Orthopedic Technician,
Dr. Raymond Sprowl, Brentwood Pet Clinic,
and Dr. Robert Olds, Orthopedic Surgeon,
as a small token of my gratitufe for their aid in saving Max's life,
and to Helen Fields for her help in preparing this manuscript.

Pepper's Ordeal

For my grandchildren,
Nicky, Chris, Emily, Natalie
and little Kyra, who grew up with Pepper.

Foreword

Every now and then one runs across a tale of great animal courage and wisdom. The animal lover within us smiles and nods, but we are not too surprised, for we love them *because* they are brave and wise.

However, the true story of Max transcends any in my experience. His indomitable will to live, his refusal, again and again, to accept defeat, and through it all his unfaltering faith in humans, must reach all of us in many different ways.

Max came back and paid his dues by opening some doors for some troubled people. However, it doesn't stop there. He will linger with many of us for all time, to bark a soft echo of encouragement when times are rough.

I am proud to know him.

BETTY WHITE
Stage, screen, and television star
Trustee, Morris Animal Foundation
National Canine Vice President
Trustee, Los Angeles Zoo

Max

The Dog That Refused to Die

In the car!" George commanded. Our two Dobermans obediently jumped into the back of the station wagon, behind a special grate separating the passengers' section from the dog's own compartment.

Max, the eldest of the two, his beautiful black coat shining like satin, settled down on the foam rubber mattress at once. He knew from experience that a long trip was ahead of him. He watched us placing suitcases in the car and knew that it meant a vacation. All during the loading of the car, he was nervous, afraid that he might be left behind. But now he could relax and take it easy. He was certain that he was going, too!

Hildy, the seven-month-old, chocolate-brown female was too excited to settle down. She playfully bit Max's ear, but he did not even growl. He just shook his head, rattling his tags, and stuck his nose between his great paws. He knew that she would settle down soon. He saw that I had thoughtfully provided Hildy with a hard ball to chew on. Soon she would start on the ball and then, bored and pacified by the rhythmic sound of the wheels and the smooth movement of the car, she too, would fall asleep.

George and I were looking forward to this little trip. He had never been to Sequoia National Park in the High Sierras, and it was years since I had been there. Besides, we had two guests visiting us—two brothers from Mexico City, Carlos and Francisco, aged twelve and eight, respectively. They were the sons of one of our best friends, an attorney. It seemed to us that the boys would enjoy a trip to the High Sierras. They had been to Disneyland and the movie studios, and we thought that a trip to the mountains would be really exciting for the two city boys.

We started early in the morning, having arranged to spend the night in a motel in Three Rivers, a small community in the foothills, planning to drive in the mountains early the following morning—the best time to enter the national forest.

It was a pleasant drive leaving crowded Los Angeles. The freeway, normally congested, was really a "free way" at this hour, for thousands of cars were moving toward the city, bringing thousands of people to work, while very few cars were on the way out. In eight hours the flow would be reversed, but by that time we would be 250 miles away in the quiet hamlet of Three Rivers.

"Do you suppose there will actually be three rivers?" Carlos asked. "I'd like to see three rivers, all at the same time!"

"Me, too!" cried the eight-year-old Francisco. He always agreed with what his older brother said.

"We'll be lucky if we find even one," I replied. "The way we have less and less rain each winter, I won't be surprised if soon there aren't any rivers left in Southern California."

"It will be nice if there is a real river," George remarked dreamily. "We'll go for a walk along the banks." Immediately the familiar phrase "go for a walk" had a galvanizing effect on the dogs. They lifted their heads, their intelligent eyes sparkling, their sharp, white teeth gleaming as eager "smiles" appeared on their elongated faces. Max barked one short, affirmative bark, which he always did when asked, "Do you want to go for a walk?"

We laughed.

"Boy, do they know those words!" George exclaimed.

"Imagine, they were fast asleep, and yet they heard us!"

"Not yet," George told the dogs as he watched them in his rearview mirror. "Soon. Now go to sleep." Obediently, Max dropped his head on his paws again, sighed deeply, and closed his eyes. Hildy stood up, turned around several times as if performing a ritual dog dance, then stretched out next to Maxie and went to sleep.

We drove along, passing small agricultural communities along the way. We stopped several times for a cup of coffee and then for lunch, letting the dogs out for a short walk on their leashes. We were not in a hurry.

It was a lovely blue and golden day, a perfect California day, becoming more perfect with every minute that we drove farther away from the smoggy city.

My husband, a doctor of psychiatry, began to sing. George was free for a few days—free of the hospital, free of patients, free to enjoy the mountains and the magnificent sequoia trees.

"Teach us some Mexican songs!" he said to the boys.

"Do you know Cielito Lindo?" asked Carlos.

"How does it go?"

"Ay-ay-ay-ay," sang Francisco in a clear, high soprano.

"Oh yes, I know that one!" exclaimed my husband as he joined the boys in a lusty rendition of the popular song.

"I know it in Russian!" I said.

"Sing it!" the boys begged. So I joined them in singing the Russian version of the lilting song.

"Let's sing it in three languages at the same time!" Francisco cried with enthusiasm. So we did, laughing at the total confusion.

The dogs lifted their heads at the sound of our singing but, hearing no familiar words, sighed contentedly and resumed their napping.

George turned off the air-conditioning and we opened the windows. The wind rushed into the car, rustling among the plastic bags containing our clothes and rocking them on their wire hangers.

We drove along miles of orange groves and apple orchards in bloom, the aroma of the blossoms wafting into the car. We were off the main road by now and were driving toward Porterville and Lindsey, two small towns in the foothills of the High Sierras.

"And to think that all of this once was nothing but a desert," said George. "Did you notice how they planted these groves? They all have irrigation ditches between the rows of trees. Their water bill must be enormous!"

* * * *

We found our motel in Three Rivers very pleasant. Our two rooms were at the back of the building facing the fast-moving river beyond a stretch of sandy shore strewn with huge boulders and smooth river stones. During the rainy season the shore must have been inundated by rushing waters, but now, late in May, the river had receded and become a rather shallow, though swift, stream.

The boys and the dogs joyfully leaped out of the car. Jumping from stone to stone, they reached the stream in no time. The dogs thirstily began to lap up the icy water rushing down from the peaks of the Sierras. Hildy waded into the water, barking foolishly and exuberantly at the little rivulets gathering and then quickly dissipating around her legs. She tried to catch the rivulets in her mouth but could not understand why all she could taste was water!

Max, the wise old boy of almost three years of age, just stood on the flat rock watching his mate. He did not like to get his feet wet and cold. He knew better than to try to catch a wave. All one would get was a nose full of water! He had tried it once or twice when *he* was Hildy's age! He was with us on one of our trips to the mountains a couple of years ago. It was very early in spring, and the ground around Lake Arrowhead was still covered with snow. Max loped happily ahead of us, joyfully biting mouthfuls of snow here and there. Suddenly, he saw a flock of ducks swimming near the landing. Without hesitation, he leaped off the pier into the icy lake.

The ducks, quacking in loud excitement, scattered in all directions, leaving Maxie thrashing wildly in the water. He made his way back to the pier, feeling very foolish.

We helped him climb up. He shook himself vigorously, sending a cascade of fine spray in all directions. The ducks regrouped and, feeling no threat, swam close to the pier, quacking as if taunting the unfortunate Max.

He ignored them haughtily. Instead, he put on an exhibition of misery for our benefit. He trembled and lifted one paw, then another, demonstrating how cold it was to stand with wet feet on the frozen ground.

We took pity on our would-be hunter.

"Okay," George said. "Let's go back to the car." Hearing his beloved word "car," Maxie forgot his discomforts and dashed ahead of us to the parking lot. He knew exactly where the car was, and he waited there, barking to hurry us on.

I used paper napkins to dry Max as best as I could, but he continued to shiver. With a sigh, George took off his own sweater and I put it on Max. Willingly, Max allowed me to pull his front paws through the sleeves as he sat on the front seat between us, still trembling but quite content.

"Don't you think that he looks rather dashing in this red turtleneck?" George asked, glancing at our noble hound.

Who knows what went through Max's mind, but ever since that time he really has hated water!

He watched Hildy now as she raced back and forth in the shallows of the stream, feeling too smart for such nonsense himself. Besides, his stomach reminded him that it was time for dinner. Max knew that five o'clock each evening was the best time of the day—eating time.

He looked at George, who was unloading the car, then at me. He gave me his paw and barked. "What do you want?" I asked, pretending that I did not know. He barked again, just once, but it had an urgent sound to it.

"Are you hungry?" Max barked again, eagerly this time for he knew that I understood him and responded with just the right words. I glanced at my watch. Right on the dot!

"George, the dogs are hungry!" I yelled to my husband. And there stood George at the door to our rooms, smiling, two dishes of dog food in his hands.

"Ready," he replied. "Dinner is served!" Maxie and Hildy did not need another invitation.

"Boy, are they smart!" exclaimed Carlos. "How did you train them?"

"We talk to them as if they were children."

"They are smarter than children!" cried little Francisco.

"Sure, they are smarter than you, loco!" laughed his

brother, giving him an affectionate poke in the ribs. The little fellow did not mind. He knew that his big brother didn't mean it. We watched them as they poked at one another, talking in rapid Spanish, calling each other names and laughing.

*　*　*　*

The next morning we were on our way to the mountains. We skipped breakfast, planning to have it at the lodge in the village, but the dogs, of course, had their feeding. Hildy was still a puppy and needed at least three meals a day, while Maxie played on our sympathy by pretending that he was starved or that he, too, was a whimpering, endearing puppy. Sometimes he would simply blackmail us by doing his tricks, knowing that we would not leave his efforts unrewarded.

His tricks included giving his paw, bringing his toys one by one, and barking on command. He also could "sit" and "come closer" by easing himself toward a person without leaving the stiff, attentive sitting position. Instead, he would slide on his behind nearer and nearer until his head would touch the person's knee. But his most spectacular attention-getters were "speaking" and "shaking hands" in foreign languages. Maxie understood and obeyed these commands in five languages: English, French, Italian, German, and Russian! When we left on vacation, he was learning his sixth—Spanish, which Carlos and Francisco were teaching him.

It took us a long time to reach the village of the giant trees, but we were not in a hurry. We enjoyed the gradual change of scenery, from the clusters of deciduous trees in the foothills with their bright green, young leaves just beginning to unfold to the darker hues of old hemlocks and cedars as we proceeded higher and higher along the winding road toward the summit. Once in a while we would spot a tall sequoia tree, a harbinger of the groves which we were soon to see.

We stopped several times to admire the view, to marvel at the beauty of the mountains, the depth of the canyons and gorges, and the crystal purity of waterfalls cascading from the mountains in ever-changing lacy patterns of splashing waters. The mist around the falls reflected the sun, and a colorful rainbow spanned the falls and the mountaintop like a magic bridge. When I was a child, I always had wanted to climb such a bridge, believing in my omnipotence.

George began to sing "Over the Rainbow," with all of us joining him again.

We passed through an open, sunlit meadow and saw several deer grazing peacefully almost at the road's edge. Hildy immediately began to bark. Her shrill, still undeveloped yelps startled the deer, and they ran into the forest.

"She always takes herself so seriously," Carlos said to George. "She thinks that because she is a guard dog and goes to obedience school, she is on duty all the time!"

"She will learn. Max will teach her. Max never barks without reason. In fact, he never does anything without a good reason," George replied.

True, Maxie always knew when to bark and how to knock on a closed door and be admitted into a room. He even learned to open a door by turning the knob with his teeth! He never chased cats at our country house, where we perpetually have crops of kittens. On the contrary, he played with the kittens and allowed them to crawl all over him, licking them with his warm, pink tongue until they would become soaking wet. Hildy, on the other hand, could not stand a cat and would chase it up the tree or onto the roof, barking furiously and preventing the frightened animal from descending from its perch.

Like two children from the same family, sharing the same love and attention but displaying completely different personalities, our dogs were distinct individuals. Hildy, a cocky, arrogant scrapper, ready for a fight, and Maxie, an intelligent, dignified guard dog who knew when to bark and when to remain silent, when to show his vicious-looking teeth in a threatening way and when to "smile."

Higher and higher we drove, following the hairpin turns that reminded us of the road in Nikko, Japan, where we had visited a few years ago.

Here and there we saw clusters of dogwood in full bloom, the large, white, delicate, waxy-looking flowers providing pleasant relief from the dark green colors of the ancient forest.

We stopped at an observation point to look over the railing. Thousands of feet below at the bottom of a deep canyon we could see the narrow ribbon of a silvery river.

Above us, reaching into the deep blue sky, were the High Sierras, monolithic and majestic, covered with tall stands of pine and oak, hemlock and cedar. Still higher up we saw huge bare rocks covered with sparkling white snow. The High Sierras. Magnificent!

We drank from a water fountain, and the dogs joined us by standing on their hind legs and adroitly catching the jets of water aimed at their mouths. Even young Hildy was able to drink this way, Maxie being an old hand at such civilized methods.

Up and up we drove, until at last we arrived at the lodge. We planned to stay in the forest until dark then spend the night at our motel in Three Rivers and be on our way home the following morning. Being Friday, it would have allowed us to reach the city in good time, long before the multitudes of people would be returning along the same freeway on Saturday or Sunday. Through long experience of traveling along California highways, we had learned when *not* to attempt to return to the city.

We had breakfast at the park cafeteria, while the dogs waited patiently in the back of the car. It was still chilly when we started walking along the trail leading into the forest. The boys ran ahead, yelling and shouting, waiting for the echo as their voices bounced off the craggy cliffs surrounding the narrow trail.

The dogs strained at their leashes, eager to run after the boys. Max and Hildy were accustomed to running freely whenever we walked with them in the mountains of San Bernardino National Forest, where we have our country home. They never strayed far, always returning to us at the first signal from the whistle that my husband wore around his neck.

For a couple of miles we led the dogs on their leashes—a difficult task with two large Dobermans on a narrow path. Finally, George suggested that we let the dogs run.

"Maybe we'd better not," I protested mildly. "They've never been here before."

"They'll be all right. They're used to being in the mountains. There's no place for them to get hurt—no traffic, nothing." George unleashed Maxie, who darted along the path like a bullet. I could not control Hildy. She went wild trying to catch up with Maxie. I unhooked her leash and she was gone. They passed the boys, not bothering to answer the invitation to play, vanishing as if swallowed by the forest.

Almost at once George and I grew uneasy. It happened often that we had the same feeling simultaneously. We wouldn't have to say a word, but we both knew what we thought or what had to be done. This time was no exception. We *felt* that the dogs must be called back. We felt that something serious had happened. Without exchanging a word we began calling the dogs. George blew his whistle, and I yelled in a special high, shrill, penetrating voice reserved for this purpose.

"Maxie! Hildy! Here, dogs!" We heard a crash among the ferns, and Hildy dashed into the path, her wet tongue hanging down like a swatch of pink velvet.

"Where is Maxie?" I asked as I attached the leash to her collar. She hyperventilated and did not make a move of protest against her leash.

George blew his whistle again. We stopped on the path, hoping momentarily to hear the sounds of Max running through the brush.

"Maxie!" the boys called. "Come back, Maxie!"

It was dark on the narrow path. The tall trees, growing close together on each side, entwined their branches over the path, creating the impression that we were inside a cool, fragrant tunnel. There was very little direct sunlight on the path, for the sun's rays had to penetrate many layers of heavy fronds of the old hemlocks and cedars. The path itself was wet. It was still covered with frost and was just beginning to thaw.

"Maxie!" I yelled. "Yoo-hoo, Ma-a-a-xie-e-e!"

Nothing. Not a fern moved.

Hildy whimpered and I patted her.

George blew his whistle in a combination of sounds that never failed to bring Maxie prancing back.

But still nothing.

We walked a little farther and stopped at a small meadow bathed in bright sunlight. I saw the tiny flowers of the wild strawberries ready to open their petals to the warm rays of the sun. In the middle of the meadow stood a young doe, looking at us with her beautiful, almond-shaped eyes. Hildy barked tentatively, but I tugged at the leash and she sat at my feet, trembling.

"Maxie!" shouted George. "Come here, boy!" The doe, startled but not afraid, slowly walked into the forest and within moments became invisible.

"Where is Maxie?" Carlos asked Hildy. She lifted her muzzle and whimpered as if trying to communicate something important. The boys petted her.

"She is trying to say something," said Francisco.

"Let Hildy call Max," Carlos suggested. "Hildy—speak!" he ordered. She looked at him, not comprehending why he wanted her to bark.

"Speak!" I said sharply. Hildy barked once.

"Speak!" George ordered. She barked again.

Again and again we made her bark, but still there was no sign of Max.

"Let's go back," George said. "Perhaps Max is waiting for us where we let him off the leash. You know how smart he is—maybe he's tired and just resting, waiting for us to come back to him instead of the other way around."

The boys stayed close to us, their exuberance snuffed out by Maxie's disappearance. "Children are intuitively sensitive," I thought.

"Perhaps Maxie *is* waiting for us," I said aloud. "I remember only a few months ago, he did just that. He retraced his steps homeward alone, over a long and confusing path. He refused to accompany George and Hildy on a hike that seemed too long to him. Maybe he's doing it now," I said. "Obedient though he is, he's also very stubborn, with a mind of his own."

We walked back all the way to the village, calling Max as we went, making Hildy bark, and blowing the whistle.

"He couldn't have got lost," George said, allaying our suppressed fears. "He's too smart for that. Besides, we let them off the leash for no more than two or three minutes!"

"Perhaps he's waiting for us at the car in the parking lot like at Lake Arrowhead," I said lamely.

George did not answer. He blew his whistle frantically several more times. It was obvious that even George was beginning to lose his usual composure.

We walked about the several different levels of the parking area, breathing laboriously in the thin air of the high altitude, our anxiety growing. We watched Hildy closely for she would have been the first to spot Maxie.

After a couple of hours of fruitless search, we decided to split our forces. George and the boys were to drive to the forest ranger station to report our missing dog. They were to drive slowly the four miles separating the village from the station, looking around in case Max somehow reached the highway. Hildy and I were to stay in the village should Maxie return there.

We sat on the curb in the shade of a giant sequoia tree. I followed every move of Hildy's eyes and hoped at any moment to see my beautiful Maxie trot into the parking place, expressing delight at finally finding his family.

"Could someone have stolen Maxie?"—the thought ran through my mind only to be discarded at once. No, Max was not the kind of a dog that people would dare to steal. Dobermans are big dogs, bred to guard and attack, and generally people are afraid of them. A full-grown Doberman with his sharp, inch-long fangs bared, a slow growl rattling deep in his throat, is an awesome sight. Max, gentle with us, was still a Doberman—a specially trained guard dog. He would not allow *anybody* to put a hand on his collar—that is, anybody but us. People would think twice before trying to steal him.

"He couldn't have got lost in such a short time, and no one would dare to steal him," I thought again. "Then—he must have been hurt. Somehow he must have been hurt and unable to let us know."

I recalled how one of our other dogs, a predecessor of Max, once hurt his foot running on the rocks on the beach near Santa Barbara. He slipped off the rock, breaking his claw, and later had to have it removed. I remembered the awful sound of scratching claws as he tried to climb up on the rock and was desperately thrashing, slipping down into the surf. My husband and our son, Ron, twelve years old at that time, had to rush to his rescue, lifting the huge weimaraner over the rocks. Tony was badly hurt as I remembered, but he was stoically silent during his ordeal. Perhaps Maxie too. . . .

George pulled into the parking area, and by his long face and the teary eyes of little Francisco, I knew that they had had no luck. They, too, glanced quickly at my side, hoping to find Maxie.

"Let's have a bite to eat and then go back on the trail," George suggested wearily. We locked Hildy in the dogs' compartment of the station wagon, leaving the windows open, and went into the cafeteria.

"I made the report," George said. "The rangers assured me that within hours someone would see Maxie and report it. They will broadcast Maxie's description on their closed circuit radio." The boys chewed their hamburgers without much gusto, their minds, like ours, occupied by various speculations of what might have happened to our dog. When we returned to the car, Hildy was nervously waiting for us. We could see that she was tense and probably worried that we would vanish like Maxie.

"Let's go," George said, snapping Hildy's leash to her special training collar. "Where's Maxie?" he asked her. She stopped short and looked around as if expecting Max to jump out of the bushes and join us.

Back on the path we went—up and down the hill, under the canopy of thick branches, the boys again running ahead. The path was dappled with the sun's rays now, the light breaking through the cover of the fringed hemlock branches like so many miniature spotlights. The sun was directly overhead now, but here in the forest it was very cool.

"Ma-a-xie-ee!" we yelled, and the echo answered, "Ma-a-xie-ee!"

We reached the meadow and the doe was there again. The meadow must have been her favorite spot. This time Hildy did not bark. She walked on the left side of my husband, obedient and subdued, as if realizing that something was very wrong and that it was not the time to be frisky.

"She misses Maxie," George said, petting her on the head. She licked his hand.

We walked farther, calling Max as we went. Finally we reached a spot where we had not been before. It was a huge, granite rock, as big as a house.

"This must be Sunrise Rock," George said. "The end of the trail." We slowly climbed to the top and looked down.

"Be careful," George warned, taking one boy by the hand. I took the other boy's hand as we peered down.

About sixty or eighty feet below us we could see some bushes and small trees. The rock itself was bare of vegetation, and the drop on the other side of it was sudden and undetectable from the path.

The same thought crossed all our minds. "Do you suppose he might have fallen off?" I finally asked.

"If he did—he is dead," George replied. "If he fell off that cliff he had no chance."

Francisco began to cry. "Poor Maxie," he sobbed. "Pobrecito."

"He had no chance," Carlos repeated, his face also bathed in tears.

We tried to find a path around the bottom of the cliff, hoping to come across some sign of our vanished dog. What sign? Perhaps the imprints of his paws? Or even his body? We did not know what else to look for. There was no path around, only the sheer drop.

It was getting dark in the forest when we returned to the main trail. We were hoarse from shouting for Maxie, our throats and mouths were parched, and the muscles in our legs were tired from so much climbing up and down the rocks.

"He's gone," George said. "We might as well face it. He's either dead or badly hurt. I can't believe that he's lost. For his sake, I hope he's dead. I don't want him to suffer—I'd rather see him dead."

"Don't say that, Uncle George," the boys begged. "Let's drive to the ranger station. Maybe someone has seen Maxie and the rangers are waiting for us. Maybe they even have Max with them already."

So we drove back to the ranger's station. A new shift had come on duty, and the rangers had heard nothing about a lost black Doberman by the name of Max. Again we made the report, describing the dog to the last detail and offering a reward of $100 to anyone who might find him.

The rangers were sympathetic and encouraging. "He'll come back. Every week we have a lost dog somewhere around here. They always come back." We were eager to believe the rangers, but deep in our hearts we knew that it was different with Maxie. He couldn't have lost his way in the forest because he was too smart for that. Besides, he was off the leash for such a brief moment. How could he have got lost in such a short time, especially when he was used to romping in the mountains since he was a pup?

George wrote a large notice about our missing dog, and we nailed it on the wall at the post office. Again we mentioned the $100 reward, asking people to call us collect, day or night, should they find Maxie. There was nothing else we could do.

We drove back to Three Rivers, seeing nothing of the magnificent scenery. We passed the groves of dogwood and the waterfalls, but we didn't look. George kept his moist eyes on the road with its hairpin curves. I knew that he was crying. Hildy was quiet in the back, and I thought that she was asleep. But when I looked back I saw that she was awake, lying with her muzzle on her outstretched paws. She looked sad and subdued, lonely for Maxie, her rubber ball all but forgotten.

Somehow the sight of my exuberant puppy looking so pathetically sad broke down my own restraint. I began to sob, painfully and deeply, admitting to myself that there was no hope for Maxie. The boys, who had been crying and sniffling for a long time, now joined us openly.

In our room at the motel, George threw himself on his bed. He, too, could not fight his grief any more and gave himself freely to its expression, not caring whether the boys thought of him being less manly for this expression of deep loss.

Hildy lifted her head and looked in surprise at her master. She had never seen nor heard a man cry. She leaped to his bed, right over his body, and placed her front paws on each of his shoulders. Then she lifted her head upward and uttered a low howl. She began to lick the tears off of his face, joining his sobbing with her whimper as an expression of her own bewilderment and loss.

I had never seen such a touching scene. This mischievous, frisky puppy joining us in our grief. Could she really have understood that we were mourning for our Maxie? I don't know. But never have I seen such an expression of sympathy from a dog as I saw that night in the motel room in Three Rivers.

It was no wonder that Hildy felt a great sense of loss. George and I had selected her as a potential mate for Max when she was only seven weeks old, shortly after we lost her predecessor, Mila. I remembered Mila and how we had acquired her in circumstances strangely similar to those in which we had just lost Maxie.

George and I were spending a weekend at Big Bear Lake. We walked around the lake, enjoying the peaceful autumn day. The air was already cool, although the sun was still shining brightly. The pine forest surrounding the lake was quiet. It was the time of the year when summer vacationers were already gone, while the ski crowd had not yet invaded the village and the surrounding countryside.

The path, covered with a thick layer of pine needles, was soft under our feet. Maxie, a puppy of six months, was running among the trees, chasing the fat squirrels who angrily chattered at him from the safety of the higher branches. Maxie's ears were still bandaged with white surgical tape after cropping. He looked like a comical black devil, with the white horns of his taped ears forming a stiff "v."

We were alone in the forest, or so it seemed, when suddenly a tiny, fluffy puppy appeared from nowhere. It followed us, playing with Maxie. They chased one another in and out of the bushes, the puppy showing no inclination to return to wherever it came from. She was a fat butterball with the most beautiful limpid dark eyes, and she couldn't have been older than eight or nine weeks.

"How did she get here?" we wondered. "It's miles away from the village. She doesn't look neglected. She's clean and fat." We yelled and whistled, expecting at any moment that someone would appear from among the trees to claim the puppy. But the forest was quiet, save for the rustle of pines.

The puppy continued to follow us, friendly and trusting. Obviously we could not leave her alone in the forest when finally we decided to turn back.

"It's getting late. . . . Let's ask in the village whose dog she is," George said. "Perhaps someone will know." We turned around and headed for the village. Suddenly, I found myself thinking that I wished we would *not* find the puppy's owners. I fell in love with the fluffy creature—so lovely, so gentle, so eager to offer herself to us. Secretly, I hoped that she was an abandoned dog and not just a lost one.

"You know, I almost wish that she would turn out to be an abandoned puppy," George said to me. "Look, just look how she plays with Maxie! I wouldn't mind at all if we were to keep her!"

I burst out laughing. "I was thinking exactly the same! You've read my mind!" I exclaimed.

As we neared the highway and the village, we put Maxie on the leash. George took off his belt and made an improvised collar and leash for the puppy. She protested the wide leather around her neck, jumping sideways, trying to slip out of the collar, but failing to do so, she gave up, walking with us obediently, fighting no more, showing her inborn intelligence.

The village was deserted, most of the summer people gone. We stopped at the grocery store to inquire about the owners of the puppy. No one knew anything about her. The service station operator knew nothing either. "Lots of people abandon their dogs at the end of summer. . . ." he said.

"Shall we ring the doorbells or shall we satisfy our conscience with what we have already done and presume that she was abandoned by some thoughtless people?" George asked rhetorically.

"We shall consider our conscience satisfied and keep the puppy," I said. "She was abandoned by her owners and she chose us to be her family. We can't betray her trust!"

"So be it," George declared.

The dogs, Maxie and his new companion, had no doubt about the outcome of our decision. Tired after the long walk and play, they cuddled together as all puppies do and were fast asleep on the rug in front of the heater.

We named the new puppy Mila, a diminutive of an ancient Russian name Ludmila, "the beloved of the people."

She grew up into one of the most beautiful dogs I had ever seen. She was fluffy as a Siberian Husky, and perhaps she was a part Husky. She also resembled a wolf. Her ears stood erect and her expressive, soft eyes were encircled with dark lines, like eye shadow. If there were equivalents in animal beauty to the movie stars—our Mila was equal to Elizabeth Taylor in her prime!

She and Maxie were inseparable. They slept together and shared the same dog house. They played and chased one another around the house, or dug deep tunnels in search of gophers in the country.

When the dogs were grown, Mila raised a litter of puppies sired by Maxie. Then, soon after the puppies were weaned, George had to attend a medical convention in Europe and I was to accompany him. We decided that the dogs would stay with the Abbotts, a fine English couple who cared for our country home. They were always glad to have Max and Mila to keep them company.

Alas, when we returned three weeks later, there was no Mila—she had been killed instantly on the highway by a speeding car.

Now our Maxie, too, seemed to be gone from our lives.

* * * *

The following morning, Friday, we drove back to the village. Our notice about Max was still at the post office. We stopped and talked to every national park employee that we met, repeating our descriptions of Max. We visited the ranger station. We walked up and down dozens of different trails, calling, whistling, all to no avail.

"Let's stay here for a couple of days," I suggested. "Tomorrow is Saturday. It will give us an extra two days to search for Maxie. We can return home on Sunday."

Friday went by with no results, and with dusk we returned to our motel. We took Hildy for a walk at the river, but she stayed close to us, showing no interest in chasing the boys or trying to catch the swift little waves and rivulets.

The next morning we returned to the park. The employees had begun to recognize us, asking solicitously whether we had had any luck.

"No, no luck," we replied. People shook their heads sympathetically. "You'll find him," they encouraged us, but there was no conviction in their voices.

Again we walked for miles. Nothing.

We stayed at the park until darkness, refusing to give up, but by Sunday we all knew that we could do no more. We loaded the car, paid our bill, and prepared to return to Los Angeles. Max was gone. Max was dead.

Still, a tiny ray of hope was flickering in my mind. "Sir, will you please call this number collect should anyone from Sequoia National Park call you about our dog?" I asked the motel manager.

"I'll be glad to. Sorry that you lost your dog. It must've spoiled your vacation," he said kindly. "I know exactly how you feel. I have a dog myself. A poodle. He's like a child to me."

Our drive back to the city was torture—many hours of driving in slow-moving traffic—just what we wished to avoid by careful planning! The beautiful orange groves, the blossoming apple orchards, the long stretches of olive groves ceased to enchant us.

"Reminds me of Spain—remember those miles of olive groves?" George asked, his voice lacking interest either in olive groves or in Spain.

"I remember," I replied. For the rest of the way we were silent. Francisco climbed into the back of the station wagon to keep Hildy company. As if understanding why he did it, she licked his face and hands and snuggled to him, both of them falling asleep, lulled by the monotonous song of the wheels.

We stopped for a meal at a roadside restaurant, and I called back to the ranger station at Sequoia National Park. What if they had found Maxie? We would turn around and dash back!

But no, no such luck.

Back at home, Hildy sniffed around the house, going from room to room searching for Maxie. That night, locked in the laundry room where she used to sleep sharing the same rug with Maxie, she cried and whimpered until I broke my own rule and allowed her to sleep in my room.

But by next day she seemed to have forgotten about Maxie. She played joyfully with the boys and chased the neighbor's cat up the tree, behaving as if nothing ever had happened to disturb our peaceful routine.

But we humans could not dismiss Maxie's disappearance that easily. We talked about him constantly, recalling every detail of his short and happy life.

"Remember how we almost got into trouble with our neighbors on account of Maxie's thievery?" George recalled fondly.

"What trouble? Tell us!" the boys begged.

"You tell them," George said. "You're the storyteller."

"Oh, okay. Well, last year, before we bought Hildy, Maxie used to be very mischievous. He used to visit our neighbors and steal things from them."

"Maxie—a thief?" Carlos, the more righteous of the two brothers, could not believe his ears.

"Yes, our noble Max was a thief," I said sadly.

"A rehabilitated thief," George corrected.

"That's true," I agreed. "His larceny was discovered just in time, and he was not allowed to pursue his criminal tendencies."

"What happened?" Francisco reminded us, interested only in the action and not in the abstract discussions of criminal tendencies.

"Well, one day we noticed strange swimming trunks on our patio. They didn't belong to George, and they were caked with dirt as if someone had dragged them through the mud. We threw them into a trash can. Then, a few days later, a bath towel appeared in the garden. Again, it was not one of ours. I asked the gardener if it was his, but he said that it wasn't. Neither did it belong to our house-keeper. I shrugged my shoulders and told her to use it as a dust cloth. A few more days passed, and another item found itself mysteriously on our front lawn—this time it was a sailing cap! No one suspected Maxie until one day I saw him staggering under the weight of a big woolen blanket that he was trying to carry in his mouth. He stumbled and struggled as he dragged it along the sidewalk and into our garage!"

The boys laughed, and even George and I smiled, recalling the capers of our larcenous dog.

"We knew then who had been bringing all those odd items home," George took over the story. "But we didn't know how to deal with the situation. We didn't even know from whom Max had been stealing!"

"You could have advertised," Francisco suggested.

"Are you stupid? They would have been sued by anyone who had ever lost anything!" Carlos objected, displaying a legalistic turn of mind.

George smiled indulgently. He liked the boys. "You're right, Carlos. We couldn't advertise. The best bet was to ask the neighbors whether any of them were missing a blanket and pretend that we knew nothing about the smaller items."

"Besides, the smaller items no longer existed," Carlos reminded. "The towel became a dust rag, and the sailing cap you gave to the gardener's son."

"And the swimming trunks you threw away," Francisco added.

"So, there was no evidence of Maxie's criminal record except the blue blanket," George continued. "We were lucky. And we were saved the embarrassment of searching for the blanket's owner. Just as we were contemplating canvassing the neighborhood, we heard an irate voice from the other side of the brick wall separating us from our neighbor. "Where in the hell is the blanket? I put it on the diving board this morning!"

The boys laughed, and we joined them.

"The next thing was to decide how to return the blanket. Should we just march into their house and present them with their blanket, admitting our dog's culpability, or should we sneak the blanket over the wall without saying anything?"

"Over the wall!" the boys shouted.

"Right! That's exactly what we did. We couldn't compromise our Maxie before the whole neighborhood, could we?"

"So what did you do?" the practical Carlos queried.

"Oh, it was a real cloak-and-dagger affair!" George puffed on his pipe as a mischievous smile of recollection curled the corners of his mouth. "We waited for the dark. Then I carried a ladder to the wall and peeked over it into the neighbor's garden. No one was there. Right under the wall there were thick bushes of azaleas planted about two feet away from the wall. I dropped the blanket down, and it landed neatly between the plants and the wall. The deed to cover up for Maxie was done."

"The next morning, after George had left for his office, I heard the shouts from the neighbor's garden," I continued, "'I've found it!' a woman was shouting."

"Where in the hell was it?"

"Right there in the bushes!"

"How did it get there?"

"I have no idea! Are you *sure* that you put it on the
diving board?"

"Of course I'm sure! I was sunbathing on it! Why would I
stick it behind the bushes? Don't be stupid!"

The boys giggled. "It must have been funny listening to
them," Carlos said.

"It sure was, although we felt a little guilty, too. Not only
did our dog steal their blanket, but he caused them to
quarrel on account of it," I said. "Oh, dear, what won't we
do for the sake of our children!"

"Your dogs, you mean," Carlos corrected.

"They are their children!" Francisco came to my defense.
"Their real children are all grown up!"

"What happened later? How did you teach Maxie not to
steal?" Carlos asked.

"Well, obviously we couldn't shame Maxie into confessing
his guilt and promising never to do it again. So instead we
raised the fence in the dog's yard a couple of feet so that he
couldn't jump over it into the neighbors' garden. It seemed
to do the trick. As he grew older, he became wiser and was
satisfied with his own toys," George explained.

"Or with your bedroom slippers," I reminded George.
"He used to carry your slippers into the doghouse."

"And chew them?" asked the boys.

"No. Just carry them into the doghouse. But when we
bought Hildy he stopped doing it."

"He had no time left for stealing," George chuckled.
"Hildy became his sole preoccupation. He had to guard his
nose from her needle-sharp little teeth."

We all fell silent, thinking of our handsome rascal, Maxie.

Carlos began to paste Maxie's snapshots in a large black
album. "It's Maxie's memorial," he announced solemnly.

"Not yet!" cried Francisco. "We might find him yet.
Maybe he's still alive."

"He is dead," Carlos pronounced with finality.

Yes, he was dead. We had to get used to that. Somehow
neither George nor I could accept the idea that Max was
lost or stolen.

* * * *

Max lifted his head and whimpered. He did not recognize his surroundings. He sniffed the air, but the scents were all unfamiliar. He smelled only the damp, decaying leaves that kept gathering from one season to another in the hollow spaces between the rocks. It was dark, and Max instinctively knew that something was wrong. He shouldn't be here among the rocks, shivering from cold, all alone. He should be somewhere else, in a warm house or a car, with his masters and his young companion, the playful puppy Hildy.

He wanted to stand up but immediately the sharp pain in his front paw made him stagger. Losing balance, he fell on his flank.

Dimly he recalled a happy outing in the woods. Two children. Not the usual members of his household, but fun to be with nevertheless. His masters and Hildy, walking along a cool path, he straining to be free of his leash. Then he remembered running after a swift squirrel and then—he had had a feeling of flying or falling down, very fast, then —nothingness.

He did not know how long he had been unconscious. Perhaps a couple of hours? A few days? How was a dog to tell the passage of time? He only knew that it had been a long time since he had had anything to eat or drink. He was starved and parched from thirst.

He tried to move again, but the excruciating pain in his front foot caused him to yelp. Max licked his paw tentatively. It felt painful even under his soft, moist tongue. He whined again, his nerves tense, hoping to hear the soothing voices of his masters who always responded to his call of distress. But all that his sensitive ears could hear now were the unfamiliar sounds of the forest at night.

Intuitively Max knew that he had to wait until morning. He whimpered like a puppy and tried to make himself comfortable, but his paw kept throbbing, making it impossible for him to settle down. He kept licking it, the salty

taste of his own blood mixing with that of saliva dripping freely from his red tongue. He finally fell asleep, his body trembling from cold and his senses numb from pain and the lack of food.

When Max awoke some hours later, the rays of the sun warmed him. He felt better, and his thoughts immediately turned to food. Was he hungry!

He yawned and stretched. At once the severe pain in his paw made itself known to him. He cried sharply, but the echo only returned his cry of anguish.

Max struggled to his feet. He knew instinctively that *he had to get home.* He did not know where his home was nor how long he had been away from it—but he knew that he had to find it.

Max limped on three legs, sniffing the ground. He searched for familiar scents but found none.

There were plenty of smells, to be sure—the frightening, foreboding scents of wild animals that raised his hackles but nothing familiar, comforting, or friendly. He sniffed the bushes, searching for the odor of his own urine. It is a sign that marks the boundaries of an animal's own territory or marks the way home. But all that he could smell was his own scent near the place where he first had regained consciousness.

Max did not know how long he had been lying among the rocks with his front foot broken, but his aching body and his empty stomach told him that it must have been a long time indeed.

He hobbled around trying to find his way out of the labyrinth of boulders and underbrush. He stopped often to rest, but each time his efforts to get up and walk again became more difficult and painful.

It must have been several days since Max had eaten. The only water that he could find was in a little brackish pool at the bottom of a large rock formation.

Max was cold at night, shivering on the frost-covered ground. In the daytime he was parched, with the sun beating down on him, drying up the little pools of thawed moisture that were his only sources of water. Still, Maxie dragged along, driven by his instinct for survival.

He encountered a family of skunks sniffing the air about them with suspicion. Max, usually so full of curiosity, barely looked at them. He was exhausted, emaciated, and dehydrated, his tongue hanging out of his mouth and his vision playing tricks on him. He breathed shallowly, ignoring the skunks. The inquisitive animals scampered away, satisfied that he represented no threat.

Various colorful birds fluttered around him as Max rested for longer and longer periods each time. The birds had no fear of the large black dog, whose coat, once shiny and sleek, was now covered with sores.

Max grew weaker every hour. Yet, with enormous effort, he continued to search for his way back home or to some human habitation. He had an unshakable trust in people. Max knew that once he reached people they would help him. He had never yet met a person who had been unkind to him. His masters, their friends, his trainer, even the veterinarians, a group of people he did not enjoy knowing, were always kind to him.

If only he could find some people!

His perseverance was at last rewarded. One day, a week or so after he was hurt, Max heard the familiar sounds of automobiles whizzing along the highway. Automobiles meant people. And people meant safety and food.

Max barked, but no one answered. He dragged himself forward with renewed energy over the forest floor covered with sharp, dry pine needles.

Every inch of his progress was torture. His body now was nothing but skin and bones covered with bleeding sores. But he limped and he crawled, driven by his powerful instinct to live. He was not going to die so close to people, so close to help!

At last he reached the highway. With the last drop of energy, he climbed the steep shoulder of the roadway and collapsed. He lay there panting, waiting for the next upsurge of strength that would give him the energy to walk along the highway until he reached people.

The cars kept passing him by, the people inside either not noticing him or not caring.

Max rested, drifting in and out of reality. At last he felt
that he was ready to try again. Painfully, he rose to his feet
and staggered across the road. Almost at once he was
struck by a car speeding along the highway. Max reeled. He
was thrown by the impact of the collision into the ditch
along the road. His tongue rolled out of his mouth, and his
eyes shut. He did not move.

"Did you hit a dog, hon?" a woman in the car asked.

"I think so," replied the man.

"Shouldn't we stop and see if we can help?"

"Naw, it was a stray. Who cares. Hell with it. Nobody
saw us."

They sped away.

* * * *

Back home in Los Angeles, we missed Maxie terribly.
Our son, a medical student now, came to commiserate with
us, bringing more snapshots of Maxie as a pup with freshly
cropped ears for Carlos' memorial album. We smiled fondly
and sadly at the pictures of a spunky puppy, his ears
wound in bandages, looking like the horns of a goat. We
looked at other pictures of Maxie playing tug-of-war with
Hildy, a tiny chocolate-brown puppy at that time. He was
so gentle with her.

We remembered also how Max had been a veritable
lover. The great passion of Maxie's life was a beautiful,
fluffy collie named Hey Girl. She belonged to our son's
friends, who lived across from us on the other side of the
golf course. The Kennons wished to breed her with another
collie and were looking forward to a litter of valuable pups.
They were still in the process of making their inquiries
through the local collie club when Maxie suddenly appeared
in their midst. Boldly, he led Hey Girl over the wall and
into the wide expanse of the golf course.

"Hey Girl, Hey Girl," the Kennons kept calling, but to no
avail.

Mrs. Kennon telephoned me, irritated with Maxie's interference in her plans for her dog.

"What can I do?" I replied. "I, too, prefer that Maxie breed with his own kind, but alas!"

That night Max reappeared, but not alone. Dirty, noticeably thinner by quite a few pounds, he jumped over the wall separating our garden from the golf course. He went straight to his doghouse, leading his guest, Hey Girl, to his dish of water. The dogs were exhausted, starved, and thirsty, so I fed them both. Then I locked them up in the doghouse and telephoned Mrs. Kennon.

"I have your dog—Max invited her to dinner. They are both asleep in his doghouse," I said.

"What?" Mrs. Kennon couldn't believe her ears. "Hey Girl visiting Max *in his doghouse?* This is too much!" she laughed, obviously forgiving me and Max for our transgressions. "And she didn't fight with him? Didn't bite him?"

"Nope. She's as gentle as a lamb."

"It's incredible! She is always very cross when she is in heat. We tried to mate her with a gorgeous collie the other day, but she bit him and wouldn't let him come close!"

"Well, she loves Maxie. He swept her off her feet!"

"What can you do? Love is blind, they always say."

"Wait, wait a minute!" I objected. "Maxie is gorgeous himself! He's the son of champions in his own right, on both sides, I may add, and I plan to show him as well!"

"Oh, I didn't mean it the way it sounded," Mrs. Kennon apologized hastily. "I know that Max is beautiful. What I meant was that he's not a collie!"

"That's true. Collie he's not," I agreed. "Anyway, let's hope that their breeds won't mix and that Hey Girl doesn't become pregnant."

But the fates willed otherwise. After another day of romancing, Hey Girl returned home. It soon became apparent that she was pregnant, and sixty-three days later she gave birth to nine black puppies. They were the spitting image of their sire, Maximillian Baron Von Haffenberg, named after my grandfather, a Russian general of long ago and a ladies' man, too.

It was impossible to register puppies of such mixed breed. They would not even be considered for registration by the American Kennel Club. So the Kennons and George and I, feeling responsible for the new lives, began our search for suitable future homes for the brood. My manicurist pledged to take one, as did our gardener. The Kennons were able to place three more, but that still left us with four puppies.

As the puppies grew, they began to acquire the characteristics of their mother's breed as well. Their coats began to look fluffy instead of sleek like Maxie's, and soon we were able to see that they resembled neither Max nor Hey Girl.

"What breed do they belong to?" my husband joked. "Are they Doberlies or Collimans?" It was hard to say, but the puppies surely were cute.

The Kennon boys, students at the University of California, took the puppies to the university fund-raising function. The puppies were auctioned for $100 each, with the money going to the student union fund.

"Not bad for a bunch of little bastards," Mr. Kennon said. "The old lady herself didn't cost us that much."

One would think that the affair between Hey Girl and Max was over. Not so. Seven or eight months later, when Hey Girl was in heat again, who but our Maxie would turn out crying at the Kennons' door!

But the Kennons were prepared. They locked up their dog and called me to get Maxie. Then they drove Hey Girl to a suburb of Los Angeles, where they had prearranged to mate her with a champion collie.

But Hey Girl was loyal to Max. She didn't want any part of the champion. She fought with him, biting him on his elegant long nose and drawing blood. The Kennons had to bring her home after paying substantial damages to the owners of her would-be mate. The moment that Hey Girl was let out of the car, she leaped over the wall, hurrying to her true love, Maxie.

Needless to say, he was ready and willing. In due course, another litter of "what-is-its" was produced, and again the two families went searching for suitable homes for the offspring. It was more difficult this time, and two of the puppies ended up at the animal shelter. But they were quickly adopted—they were just too cute to be overlooked. After remembering Maxie's exploits we were glad that he had truly enjoyed himself while he was alive. We still wondered, though, how his absence would affect Hildy. She seemed to develop a new personality—she became less rambunctious and more obedient. She was not missing Maxie the way we did, but she knew that something had changed in her short, happy life. She stayed close to my side.

"Do you suppose she saw Maxie getting killed?" we kept wondering.

Every other day I called the ranger station.

"Any news about Max?"

"No, ma'am. We'll let you know if we hear anything."

"Stop calling them," my husband urged me when two weeks had passed without any news. "Max is gone. Dead."

"I know, but—"

I continued to call the rangers, but now I did my phoning after George left for his office. I knew it was foolish. The rangers probably thought that I was crazy, but I could not reconcile myself to the idea that Maxie had just vanished. Deep in my heart I hoped that Maxie was found by some kind soul and perhaps was waiting for us to pick him up.

However, as the days went by I began to admit even to myself that George was right and that Maxie was gone forever.

*   *   *   *

Maxie regained consciousness some hours later. He lay in a ditch along the road, the flies buzzing over his open sores. He felt pain all over his wasted body, but still he tried to stand up. He had a vague recollection of his long trek toward the highway and his struggle to climb over the shoulder of the road.

As Max braced himself to get up on his feet, he suddenly realized that his right hind leg and his hip were immobile. He looked back at his leg and saw it twisted, hanging down helplessly. The suffering dog had a broken hip and hind leg! He licked his injured leg, unable to stand up. Wise beyond his years, Max knew that he had reached the final chapter in his fight for life. He dropped his head on his outstretched paws, waiting to drift into the blessed state of semiconsciousness, when one is spared the feeling of pain, the frustration of uncertainty, and the all-enveloping fear of death, be one a human being or an animal.

Still, Max did not die. Several more days must have passed before he finally ventured out of the ditch. All around him he could smell the presence of people. From time to time he heard the shrill voices of children playing somewhere nearby. Smells of campfires and cooking drifted toward him, renewing his quest for survival. Max knew that there must be a camp nearby. He was almost there.

If only he could get close enough to people! Max felt that his life was ebbing away fast. If he didn't reach people, he knew he had no chance to live. Max barked, but his voice was weak and no one heard him.

He gathered the last remnants of his strength and, using his broken front paw despite excruciating pain, stood up. He hobbled on three legs to the other side of the highway, crossing it at night because he sensed that the danger of being hit by a car would be less at that time.

Once on the other side, he hobbled the other two miles that separated the camp from the road. Exhausted by his effort, he fell down again, this time within sight of the campers. Max could move no more.

Hours later, as another night was fast approaching, Max gathered enough strength and limped toward a group of children playing in front of a camper.

"Look at this poor doggy," a young boy cried. "He is just skin and bones!" Max tried to wag his short tail to show that he was friendly. The boy petted him, noticing Maxie's tags.

"Get away from that dog!" a woman yelled from the back door of the camper, throwing an empty beer can at Maxie.

It hit him on his broken hip. He yelped shrilly and desperately and limped into the bushes, collapsing near a sequoia tree stump.

"The dog probably has rabies and he may be dangerous," the woman continued to yell, ordering the children into the camper.

"What's all this ruckus about?" A fat, sleepy man appeared at the door of another camper, rubbing his eyes with the back of his fists. "Where's this mad dog?"

"Right there, in the bushes," the woman replied, pointing to the spot where Maxie had disappeared into the thicket.

"I'll get him!" the man exclaimed, his sleepiness all but gone as he dashed into the camper for his shotgun.

In a moment he reappeared, his loose suspenders now firmly pulled over his shoulders and crisscrossing his back, his huge belly dancing inside his dirty, baggy trousers.

"We don't want no mad dogs around these here premises," he muttered angrily as he emptied his shotgun into a cluster of underbrush.

"I wish I could see where the hell he is—this mad dog." He reloaded his gun and shot into the bushes again.

"He was right there. You probably got him," the woman chattered shrilly. "Right there, in the bushes. Ain't it something! A mad dog in the park! They ought to do something about it. It ain't right to have mad dogs running around a public park!"

The children crowded at the doors of both campers afraid to come out, yet fascinated and burning with desire to examine the dead mad dog. But it was too dark, and they knew that they had to wait until morning.

"Did you touch him?" a girl asked the boy who had seen Max first, her eyes round with excitement.

"Sure," the boy said. "I petted his head."

"Did he bite you?"

"Of course not! He was friendly," objected the boy. "I know that he belonged to somebody. He had a red collar on, with tags. His name is Max; it was on his tag."

"I say he was dangerous," insisted the woman. "I've never seen a scurvier looking dog in my life! He was probably abandoned by his owners because he was mad. He looked vicious. All Dobermans are vicious. I would never trust a Doberman. They turn on their masters. I saw a movie once where a Doberman turned on his owner and tore him to pieces." She kept rattling on as the children listened, their eyes wide with the wonder of their miraculous escape from the jaws of the mad dog.

* * * *

Max heard the blast of the shotgun, and a shudder ran through his emaciated, exhausted body. He was too weak to crawl away. He stayed where he was behind the huge, hundred-year-old sequoia stump as if knowing that it offered him the best protection. Then the second blast shattered the silence of the forest.

He heard people's voices, but they sounded loud and unfriendly. Max knew that the people in the campers were his enemies. He knew now that it was dangerous for him to remain in their vicinity. Yet he stayed, for he recalled one person—a child—who had been kind to him. Something made him want to see this person again. The child reminded Max of the boys who had been with his masters a long time ago, driving in a car with his friend Hildy. Maxie wasn't sure when it all had happened, but he had a dim recollection of a feeling of peace and contentment. This child, who petted him, reminded him of those happy times.

It was another very cold night in the woods, and the ground began to stiffen under a thin layer of frost. Max licked the frosty crust, and it made him feel a little better by moistening his parched mouth. He waited until it was completely dark and he could hear no sounds from the campers. He knew now why he remained so close to the unfriendly people. It wasn't only the boy. Wherever there were people, there was food. An unfinished hamburger, half a cookie, a chicken bone. Always something. His instinct urged him to scavenge around the campers.

Max pulled himself up. Painfully, he limped back, closer to the campers. He sniffed at two garbage cans but could not lift their lids, and he was too weak to turn the cans over. Suddenly, Maxie must have realized that he had no more strength. For the first time since he had fallen off the cliff, he became completely apathetic.

During the night he crawled as far away from the campers as he could. Sick and hurt as he was, Max still knew when he wasn't wanted.

With the first rays of the warm sun the ground began to thaw. Maxie opened his eyes and shut them at once. The sun was too bright for his inflamed, dry eyes, yet he thought that he saw something—something that he was searching for so desperately.

Right in front of him were several rough-hewn cabins and cleanly swept sidewalks. He sniffed the air and again smelled people. Different people. People in houses, like home. There was no scent of oil and gasoline, which he had smelled at the trailer camp.

Then he tensed. His experience of the previous night taught him that not all people were his friends. Max was wary now. He waited, listening for harsh, unfriendly voices, but there were none. He saw people move in and out of the cabins, and he called out to them, but his voice must have become so weak that no one heard him. He tried to pull himself up and crawl closer to the cabins, but no strength remained in his body.

The day passed slowly for the suffering dog. Max drifted in and out of consciousness, barely aware of the passage of time. Another cold, brilliant night slowly descended upon the mountains and the giant trees. Max was dying.

As the full moon finally ascended, bathing the woods and the nearby cabins in its soft, cool light, Max became aware of still another danger. His keen ears picked up the sound of a pack of coyotes. Normally Max would have answered their call with his own threatening bark. But now he just whimpered, hoping instinctively that the wild creatures would stalk some other prey. Still, the howls kept coming closer as the coyotes followed Maxie's scent. They knew that their prey was injured and followed the smell of blood dripping from Maxie's injured feet. They were brazen creatures, often boldly scavenging near human habitats, unafraid of anything but the loud discharge of gunshot.

They came to the clearing before the cabins, five of
them, ghostly apparitions in the silvery moonlight. Their tails
were bushy, almost like foxes' tails not yet having shed their
long, winter hair. Their eyes reflected the moon, gleaming
phosphorescently and menacingly.

They circled the dying dog slowly, not ready yet to attack
but narrowing the orbit of their approach, boldly ignoring
the presence of human habitation.

Max bared his teeth and growled, but only a rattling
sound came out of his weakened throat. The coyotes knew
that they had an easy prey. It could be theirs whenever
they wished. They howled again, one after another. Then
they pounced on Max, yelping like young dogs with
excitement.

"Damn it, I'm gonna get them once and for all!" a man
swore inside one of the cabins. He switched on the elec-
tricity, and powerful lights flooded the clearing before the
cabins. The sudden brightness frightened the coyotes, and
they scampered in all directions.

Max wanted to bark, to let the man know that he was
near and that he needed help, but no sound came from his
dry throat. He lay panting shallowly, unable to lift his head.
The man left the floodlights on throughout the night. The
coyotes dared not return.

In the morning, the warm sun somewhat revived Maxie
once more. He opened his eyes and saw the cabins. So
near! If only he could crawl a little closer!

He heard light footsteps on a path leading from the
parking area. A young girl dressed in blue jeans and a
Mexican blouse slowly walked along the path with an
armload of bed linen, whistling as she went. She had a
friendly, freckled face framed by long, brown hair. Maxie
could smell the fresh scent of her soap, and it reminded him
of home. He whimpered and the girl stopped.

"Oh, you poor miserable creature," she said softly,
placing the linen on a wooden bench and bending over
Maxie. "What happened to you, boy? Are you hurt?" Maxie
tried to lift his head and nuzzled her hand. He was too
weak to lick her hand properly.

"Poor, poor baby," the girl crooned. "You are starved!" She looked at Maxie's tag and read aloud. "MAX. If lost— please notify Dr. and Mrs. George Wayne. REWARD." Then followed our telephone number.

"You poor boy," she said. "You must've been lost. Stay here, I'll bring you something to eat." She picked up her linen and ran toward the office.

Max did not want to let her out of his sight. It was the first time in three weeks that he had heard the sound of a friendly human voice. Sick and almost dead as he was, he still recognized the familiar words "stay" and "eat." He managed to utter one hoarse bark to let her know that he appreciated her concern, but he did not want her to leave him. He strained trying to get up and found that he had no muscles left to help him lift his body. He was weaker than a blind puppy. He whimpered pitifully, watching the back of the disappearing girl.

She turned around quickly, and her heart went all out to the suffering dog.

"Don't worry, Max," she said, calling him by his name. "I promise, I'll be right back."

The sound of his own name quieted Maxie. Somehow he trusted her and knew that she would return.

* * * *

It was almost eight o'clock in the morning of June 11 when the phone rang in our home in Los Angeles, three weeks and one day since Max's disappearance.

"This is long distance. Will you accept a call from Sue Harrison?" the impersonal voice of the operator intoned when I picked up the receiver.

"Sue Harrison?" I repeated and turned quizzically to my husband, who was reading the paper and drinking his coffee. He shrugged his shoulders.

"I don't know any Sue Harrison," he said.

"Do you know Sue Harrison?" he turned to Carlos and Francisco, who were eating their ham and eggs at the kitchen table.

"No," the boys shook their heads. "We don't know anyone of that name."
"Ask where she's calling from," said George.
"Where is the call from?" I asked the operator.
"Sequoia National Park."
Before she finished I was already shouting into the receiver, "Yes, yes, of course we accept! Put her on!"
Sue Harrison came on the line promptly.
"Did you lose a dog?" she asked without preliminaries.
"Yes, yes!" I cried. "Do you know where he is?"
"What's his name?"
"Max!" I shouted. "Is he alive?"
"Yes," said Sue. "He is alive, but barely. He is badly hurt."
By this time, George was on the extension line in the library. I was too shaken to talk. I listened on my end of the extension in the kitchen, crying, laughing, then crying again.
"What happened?" the boys wanted to know. I waved them toward my bedroom, where they picked up another extension.
"Yes, Max is alive, but barely," Sue was saying. She went on to describe briefly how she had found Maxie and about his pitiful condition.
"He has two broken legs and is emaciated beyond description," she was saying. "I don't think he can survive much longer." She had fed him, sharing her sandwich, and given him fresh water to drink, but she felt that the dog was too far gone.
"Everybody here says that he should be put to sleep," she was saying, "put him out of his misery. But I think he has a chance. If he were my dog I would try to save him."
George begged Sue to take Maxie to the nearest veterinarian hospital, perhaps in Porterville, for it would take us at least six to seven hours to reach Sequoia National Park.
"We want to save him!" he kept repeating. "We must!"
If Maxie was that badly hurt, every hour counted. We knew that we had to hurry. Without medical help, every extra hour could become his last one.

Sue agreed to take the dog to the veterinarian. She told us that she worked as a housekeeper at the park and could not get away that day, but her girlfriend, Jo, volunteered to drive the injured Maxie down the mountain and into the vet's clinic. She told us something about her friend so that we would recognize her. I did not listen. My heart was pounding with excitement.

Quickly we called telephone information and inquired about animal clinics in Porterville.

One doctor was on vacation; another did not care to wait for our arrival possibly after office hours. Fortunately, we found a kind, understanding person in Dr. Merrill, who agreed to wait for us and give Maxie first aid as soon as he was delivered to the clinic.

We phoned Sue back at the park, giving her the name and address of the doctor. That arranged, George had to cancel his own appointments. He rushed to the hospital, saw two or three acute patients, then asked his secretary to cancel the rest.

As good luck would have it, only one more patient was scheduled, and he happened to know about Maxie's disappearance. When he heard that the dog had been found, he volunteered to reschedule his appointment so that we could go after Maxie at once.

Meanwhile, Carlos and Francisco, on their own initiative, made a long distance call to Mexico City, begging their parents to allow them to stay with us for a few more days.

"We must see Maxie, we must have him checked into an animal clinic and help to care for him when he is allowed to return home." The boys had no doubt that Maxie would be all right, now that he was found.

"It was a miracle," they kept saying to their parents. "We prayed for a miracle—and it happened. We must be with Maxie to make sure that he is well! We knew all the time that he would be found. We prayed for him."

Neither we nor the boys' parents could raise any objections to such a complete demonstration of faith.

"Of course you may stay longer," their parents finally said, "if Uncle George and Aunt Kyra don't mind."

"Of course we don't mind," we replied, reassured by the children's unshakable belief in Maxie's ultimate recovery.

I placed several meat patties and a gallon of water into an ice chest for Maxie, and then we were off. By five o'clock in the afternoon we arrived in Porterville.

I don't remember anything about our driving, only the feeling of elation that we were about to see our wonderful, marvelous, valiant Maxie! We did not stop to eat along the way. George and I were too excited to eat, while the boys were happy to munch on cookies, apples, and candy bars. No one cared for food—only for time, the time that it would take to see Maxie again.

We found the animal clinic located in a pleasant rural section of town, in the midst of orange groves. The air was fragrant from the blossoms, the earth hot and pungent under the warm California sun. We parked in the shade of an old giant olive tree to keep Hildy comfortable.

With trepidation we entered the clinic.

Dr. Merrill was examining a patient, a grey Persian cat. We heard the cat hiss and spit. The doctor talked to her in a soothing voice, and the cat quieted down. The people sitting around his waiting room with various pets on their knees or at their feet smiled knowingly.

"Dr. Merrill is very good," said an elderly Mexican woman with a puppy on her lap. "He speaks to the animals." The people around the room nodded their agreement.

"Dr. Wayne and his wife are here from Los Angeles," the receptionist called to Dr. Merrill.

"I'll be with you in a moment. Please wait in my office," said the doctor.

We entered his office. The receptionist brought us two cups of coffee and offered lollipops to the boys. Presently, the doctor, a young, good-looking man in his thirties, entered the room, wiping his hands on a paper towel.

He shook hands with us and sat down behind his desk. "We had X rays done on your dog," he said. "His left front paw has several broken toes, and his right femur is shattered in several places. But the most serious is his general condition. He is dehydrated and emaciated almost beyond belief. By the way, the young lady who brought him in— she is still here, waiting for you."

"May we see Maxie?" George asked.

"But of course!" He took us to the back of the building, where there were two levels of cages. Almost all of them were occupied by sick animals. On the lower level, in one of the largest cages, was our Max.

Or was it Maxie's shadow? Maxie's skeleton? Surely this pile of bones covered by a dull, lifeless coat full of bleeding sores was not our elegant, handsome Maxie, the son of champions, the paragon of canine beauty?

He was lying on his side, panting shallowly. Every one of his ribs stood out like the underpinnings of an unfinished keel of a sailing vessel. His tongue, hanging lifelessly out of his closed mouth, looked gray instead of its usual vivid pink. The sticky saliva bubbled at the corner of his mouth. His eyes were shut, and were it not for his shallow breathing he looked dead.

"Maxie!" George called him gently. "What happened to my good boy?"

The dog opened his eyes, and we knew that he recognized us. He whimpered and tried to wag his stump of a tail. It barely moved. His whole hip was shattered, and the muscles of his entire body, and especially of his right hind leg and hip, were practically atrophied.

Dr. Merrill opened the cage and we bent over Maxie, all of us crying. Happy tears for his deliverance were mixed with the bitter ones of sympathy and compassion.

Max licked our hands with his dry, sandy tongue, uttering pitiful little cries of recognition, letting us know that he, too, was happy to be reunited with his family.

"We gave him a shot of antibiotics," the doctor was saying, "and of course, we fed him and gave him water."

"Was he able to eat?" I asked.

"And how! Nothing wrong with his appetite!"

"What would you advise, Dr. Merrill? Has he a chance for survival?" George asked. "We want to save this dog."

Dr. Merrill closed the cage. "Come with me to my office. Before you decide, I want you to see the X rays of your dog's injuries."

Passing through the reception room we saw a young girl in blue jeans with a bandage around her shoulders and neck. It was Jo. I remembered dimly that Sue Harrison had said something about Jo, mentioning that she had just broken her collarbone. I had been so preoccupied thinking of getting Maxie to the vet that I had not really paid much attention to what Sue had been saying. Now I knew. Sue had been telling us about Jo breaking her collarbone in a freak bicycle accident. And here she was, this pretty, curlyheaded girl from Minnesota, whose broken collarbone must have been painful, yet she drove the long, winding mountain road to bring our dying dog to the clinic!

I embraced the girl and, following an impulse, kissed her. "I can't tell you how grateful we are to you for saving our Max!" I said.

"It's not me. I just brought him here. It's Sue who found him and made all the arrangements," she replied, modestly.

We wanted to give her a check for the $100 promised as a reward for finding our dog, but Jo flatly refused the money.

"No, no, no," she said. "Sue and I have discussed the reward, and we decided that you would need every penny of it to pay for his doctor bills. We both love animals, and we understand how you must have felt when you lost Max." She was determined that we did not owe them anything for saving our dog.

Finally, George persuaded her to accept a token of ten dollars to cover at least the gasoline expenses of her trip to Porterville. Fortunately, I had packed a gift for Sue that I intended to give her in addition to the reward money. It was a colorful leather shoulder purse from Mexico that I had bought last year and kept as a possible present for some friend's birthday or as a Christmas gift. I gave it now to Jo for Sue, as a token of our gratitude.

"Good luck with Max!" she smiled as she started her car. "He is a wonderful dog; I hope you'll be able to save him!" She was gone.

"What's your last name?" I shouted, but Jo did not hear me.

We returned to the doctor's office.

"It's unbelievable! The girls absolutely refused the money!" I said shaking my head in wonder. "They refused $100!"

"It kind of renews your faith in the human race, doesn't it?" Dr. Merrill chuckled.

"It surely does," George agreed. He was looking at Max's X rays, tracing the fragmented bone clearly visible on the large sheet of negative.

"If he were my dog, I wouldn't use euthanasia," said Dr. Merrill. "I would try to save him."

"That's exactly what I wanted to hear!" George exclaimed. "I want to save this dog! He deserves to be given a chance after all he's been through. Imagine, three weeks without food or water, with two badly broken legs and God knows what other injuries! This intelligent, wonderful animal mustn't be destroyed. My wife and I, we'll save him, we'll nurse him back to health!"

"And we will help," cried Carlos and Francisco almost in unison.

"Unfortunately, we don't have proper facilities to care for him," Dr. Merrill continued. "Max needs special orthopedic surgery, 'plating' as we call it. We don't have it here. But I can recommend an excellent animal hospital in Los Angeles where they have orthopedic specialists. We have dealt with them several times before in some complicated cases, and they were always very good."

He called the clinic for us to advise them to expect us with our dog within a few hours.

We paid the bill for Maxie's first aid and the X rays, then George carried the dog to the car.

"He weighs no more than a three-month-old puppy," George said. "What happened to you, boy? You used to have muscles of steel."

George placed Max gently in the back of the station wagon on a clean, soft blanket spread over his foam rubber mattress. Hildy, switched from the back of the car to the passenger's seat in the middle, did not object. She settled herself between the boys, and then, sticking her long muzzle through the grate separating the dogs' compartment from the rest of the station wagon, she sniffed at Maxie and licked his nose. Maxie barely lifted his eyelids.

"Goodbye, Dr. Merrill, thank you for your help," we said.

"Let me know how Maxie's doing," the doctor smiled, waving us on our way. "Get him to the clinic as fast as you can. He is very weak."

George started the engine.

For the fourth time within a month we were driving along the same country road bordered on both sides by endless fruit orchards. The blossoms were gone now. The trees had the uniformity of well-trained regiments lined up for a parade. There was practically no traffic on our side of the road. Most people were now safely home from work and were having dinner and watching television. Many cars were moving from the opposite direction—people leaving Los Angeles and Bakersfield on their way to a weekend in the mountains—but that traffic didn't affect our progress.

George drove fast, exceeding the speed limit of fifty-five miles per hour, but we had no choice. Maxie was sinking fast.

We stopped before getting on a freeway and checked him. He could not lift his head. I washed his face and mouth with cool water, noticing that his gums looked grey and his teeth, once sparkling white and menacingly sharp, now were covered with a yellowish, odorous film.

"We must hurry," I said on the verge of tears again. "I think he is dying."

"Not my Maxie," George exclaimed fiercely. "Not after all he's been through. No, my Maxie is not going to give up when help is so near!" He stepped on the accelerator.

Hildy tried to lick Maxie through the metal grill, but Max was oblivious to her attempts of welcoming him back. He breathed fast, his bare rib cage moving up and down like a set of bellows.

"I think we're going to get a ticket," George said, looking at the rearview mirror. He maneuvered the car to the right side of the freeway and stopped on the shoulder of the road.

A California Highway Patrol car pulled up behind us.
"May I see your driver's license, please?" a young patrol-
man came to our window. George mutely handed over his
license.
"Did you know that you were speeding, sir?" he asked
politely.
"Yes, officer, I am aware of it," George replied.
"Officer, we had to hurry!" Francisco interrupted, his
voice full of tears. "We have a dying dog in the back. We
must take him to the vet in Los Angeles or he will die!"
The officer looked at Francisco, surprised at his outburst.
He was young, perhaps the same age as our son, Ron.
"Just take a look in the back!" I joined, encouraged by his
kind young face. "Just take a look at our poor dog!"
George came out of the car and went to the back of it,
the officer following. George lifted the rear door of the car,
and the patrolman peered in.
"You poor beast," he said softly to Maxie. "What happened to you? Were you hit by a car?"
"He was lost for three weeks in the mountains, in the
forest," the boys hurried to inform the officer, instinctively
feeling the presence of a kindred soul. "He has two broken
legs, a broken hip, and he is practically starved to death.
We are trying to save his life by taking him to the animal
hospital in Los Angeles."
"That's why I was speeding," George said. "All I have on
my mind is saving this dog."
"I don't blame you," the young patrolman said. "I have a
dog myself. A Labrador retriever. I understand how you
feel. I'll tell you what—follow me closely. I'll take you as
fast as I can to the boundaries of my territory. Then I'll
radio to my buddies along the freeway to let you pass. I'll
be breaking the law, but sometimes one has to do it to save
a life. Follow me." He returned to his car and veered in
front of us. He turned on the revolving red light on the roof
of his car and waved for us to follow.
"I can't believe it!" George exclaimed. "A cop helping us
to break the law so that we could save Maxie's life!"

"God bless him!" I thought. "May he, his Labrador retriever, his wife, his children, if he has any, live happily for
ever and ever!"

"Thank you, officer!" the children yelled as the young
policeman smiled at them.

We sped after the patrolman, passing car after car, following closely behind his flashing light. In about forty
minutes, he switched off his light and motioned us to continue as he changed lanes bearing to the right.

We understood that he had come to the boundaries of his
territory. I waved to him and blew him a kiss as we passed
him. He grinned and waved back and drove away at the
next freeway exit.

"And we didn't even ask his name!" I lamented.

"Shall we continue to drive faster than the speed limit?"
George asked tentatively.

"Yes," I said resolutely. "The patrolman said that he
would radio ahead to his buddies."

"He will!" the boys cried from the backseat. "He's a nice
guy!"

"What the hell, let's try it!" George said keeping his speed
steady at sixty-five.

We drove for another forty or fifty minutes, passing car
after truck, getting ever nearer to the city and the clinic.
Max still breathed fast. Were it not for his breathing, he
looked dead.

Far ahead of us we saw a long line of vehicles moving at
a lesser speed behind a police car that was pacing them.

"Shall we take a chance and overtake them and risk
getting a ticket?" George asked rhetorically, answering
himself with, "Yes, we'll take a chance."

Steadily he drove, ten miles per hour faster than the
convoy. We began to pass the cars, one by one, the drivers
reacting to our gall with various degrees of puzzlement at
our behavior or with smug expressions of righteousness.
They were all good, law-abiding citizens, while we were the
outlaws who were about to get our comeuppances. I was
sure that many of them were waiting with glee to see the
pacing patrol car chase after us.

We overtook them all, until we pulled abreast of the leading patrol car.

There were two men in the car, the older one driving. They glanced at us, first in amazement at our daring to go by them so brazenly, then they said something to one another, and the younger one checked a slip of paper on his dashboard. It all happened so fast, but I thought that I saw them smiling at us. Yes, they did smile, and the younger one made a peace sign with his two fingers! I saw it in my visor mirror.

"He did radio his buddies!" the boys cried triumphantly. "We knew he would!" For the second time that day I heard the phrase, "It renews your faith in the human race." As George said it, an amused smile crossed his tired face.

Twice again we passed the patrol cars, and each time we were waved on.

"Do you suppose he radioed our license number and the description of the car to all the highway patrolmen along the freeway?" I asked.

"It certainly looks like it," replied George.

It was dark by the time we reached Los Angeles, but we reached it in a record time of less than three hours!

* * * *

The West Los Angeles Veterinary Medical Group was situated in a new building with all the latest conveniences of a modern hospital. Both my husband, a doctor, and later our son, almost a doctor, commented that they would not mind practicing in such a fine facility. It had its own operating rooms, X ray department, pharmacy, laboratory, several examining rooms, the latest computerized filing equipment, and many other features undoubtedly unseen by outsiders. It was spotlessly clean, and it was staffed by several young veterinarians of various specialties. It operated on a twenty-four-hour basis, with an emphasis on emergency medicine.

A young woman, Dr. Dore Ozdy, was on duty.

"Oh, you poor, poor creature!" she exclaimed when George and a young husky attendant lifted Maxie onto the examining table. "You are on your last legs!"

"Figuratively and actually speaking," my husband commented.

"What happened to him?" Briefly we described what we knew about Maxie's ordeal.

"Do you want to put him to sleep, or do you want to try and save him?" Dr. Ozdy asked.

"Of course we want to save him!" we all cried in unison. Then George elaborated: "We feel that we want to do everything that is possible to save his life and to restore his health. This dog means a lot to us. We have had him since he was seven weeks old. We trained him, we nursed him through his unpleasant weeks of ear healing after the ears were cropped, we love him. He's a remarkable dog—he understands thirty or thirty-five different words. We can't desert him now, when he really needs us, after he has struggled for his life with such valiance!"

"He even understands Spanish!" Francisco volunteered.

"And French and German and Russian!" Carlos interrupted, unwilling to be overshadowed by his sibling.

"Must be a remarkable dog," the veterinarian smiled at the boys.

"We can't put him to sleep!" I joined my husband. "After this dog fought so bravely to survive, we must give him a chance to live." For us, saving Maxie's life had become an obsession, a symbol of the value of life itself. "Maxie is more than a pet to us. He is a friend. A child."

"I understand perfectly," the doctor said as she petted Maxie's head. "If he were my dog, I would make the same decision. But you realize, of course, that he might be a cripple forever? Looking briefly at his X rays, it seems to me that he will have to have a metal pin or a plate in his hip."

"We don't care if he is a cripple!" I exclaimed. "We love him for what he is!"

"So—he won't win any blue ribbons," my husband said. "He still is a champion with me!"

"He surely is," the doctor agreed. "If he only could tell us exactly what happened to him. What a tale it would be!" She took Maxie's temperature. It was normal.

"It's a good sign," she said. "Tomorrow we'll take more X rays. We'll put him on antibiotics and anabolic steroids and on a special high-protein diet. We have to build up his resistance before we attempt surgery. We will also check his blood and urine."

"What about his sores?" I asked.

"We'll clean them and put some special salve on them. They'll heal. The sores are one of his lesser problems. We'll do everything for him that modern veterinary medicine has to offer. But it will be very costly. Multiple surgeries, anesthesia, X rays, lab work, maybe even intensive postoperative care."

"I realize it," my husband said. "But I want this dog saved. At all cost." We petted Maxie as the attendant carried him away.

"The next few days will be crucial," Dr. Ozdy said. "Keep in touch with us by phone, but I would advise you not to visit him. We'll keep him under mild sedation so that we can run a series of tests on him. We'll let you know if anything unusual happens, so try not to worry."

"Alright, doctor. Thank you." We left the hospital.

* * * *

Max was placed in a large cage with layers of clean newspapers on the floor. A metal cup full of fresh water was attached to the inside of the cage at a level where the dog could drink without standing on his feet.

Thirstily, Max lapped the water. Then he closed his eyes again. He felt peaceful. Although his masters and the boys had left, somehow he understood that he was not abandoned and that someone else would be taking care of his hurting, battered body.

He felt a sharp prick of a needle in his neck as the doctor gave him an injection to relax him and to relieve him of pain. After that, he slept until morning.

The next day, the team of doctors and attendants began their fight for Maxie's life.

He was fed vitamins and antibiotics and steroids and intravenous fluids to bring his blood chemistry back to its necessary balance. His extremities were x-rayed, and the films were read. He was fed a special diet in small portions several times a day. His temperature and bodily functions were monitored, and the attendants watched over him twenty-four hours a day.

Maxie submitted meekly to the needles and the X rays, as if understanding that the people who hovered around him were his friends. He probably did not miss us for he was in a constant state of semisedation. But we missed him and worried over him greatly.

We called the hospital daily, getting complete reports on his progress from the girls at the reception desk, sympathetic to Maxie's plight. Our friends teased that we ought to send flowers to the hospital.

"Never mind," George was saying. "Everyone is pulling for Maxie. He is becoming a 'cause celebre.' "

On the fifth day after his admission to the hospital, Max finally regained enough strength to undergo surgery. We called the hospital twice, but he was still in the operating room. Finally, after six hours of surgery, our Maxie was back in his cage. We were told that we could visit him the following day.

George had to leave that day for a medical meeting in Florida. The boys and I took him to the airport, and then we met our son Ron, who also wanted to see Maxie. The boys had a present for Maxie—a pattie of lean ground beef.

The attendants led us into the ward. Every cage was occupied. In one cage we saw a fluffy Siberian husky wearing a huge, round collar that looked like a high, starched collar of Queen Elizabeth I. The dog was somewhat embarrassed wearing this cumbersome contraption, but it prevented the animal from licking and pulling out the stitches on her belly. Another dog sported a cast up to his shoulder, while still another had bristling metal sutures on its neck.

And then we saw our Max. His left front leg was in a splint up to his shoulder, and his right hip and the right hind leg were encased in an elaborate bandage that encircled his abdomen. The fur on the hind part of his body was shaved off, and the skin beneath looked dry and grey and lifeless. He recognized us and whined. We knelt at his cage and called his name.

"Look what we brought for you, Maxie!" the boys said. "Are you hungry?" Hearing the familiar word "hungry," Maxie gave us a single bark, his usual reply to this question. It was a weak bark, far from his usual ringing, assertive sound, but it was a bark nevertheless, an answer.

"He did not forget!" I exclaimed, delighted with Maxie's reaction. All these past days George and I had speculated and worried whether Maxie's mental condition had deteriorated along with his physical state. Would he be able to understand us as before, when by the tone of our voices alone or even a hand signal, our highly trained dog had known exactly what was expected of him? Would he obey us? Or was he so badly hurt physically that his mental capacity had suffered irreparable damage?

His little feeble bark at the right time, sedated as he was, made us sure that Maxie was his own smart, dear self again and that nothing was wrong with his mental ability.

He gobbled up the meat, not caring to chew it. He licked Ron's hands, recognizing him also, although he did not see him too often. Ron, being a young man of twenty-three and almost a doctor himself, no longer lived with us.

It was time to go. We thanked the doctors and the attendants for all they had done for Maxie.

"Oh, Maxie is our favorite," one of them said. "He became the symbol of courage to us. We all pull for him. He'll be OK, he's a tough guy! He must have been in perfect condition to be able to come out alive from such an ordeal!"

"Oh yes. He used to be the most muscular dog I've ever seen!" Ron said.

"He was as fast as a racing dog," Carlos added.

"He'll race again. Maybe on three legs only, but barring complications, he'll race again!" The attendant ruffled

Carlos' hair in a friendly gesture. "He might not win any races, but he'll race again, you'll see!"

*   *   *   *

Max stayed at the hospital for two more weeks. When we finally brought him home, a telegram was waiting, addressed to Maxie Wayne. "Welcome home Maxie," it said. It was signed by our friends, Dr. and Mrs. Goldsmith, and their three children. Then another telegram came— from Mexico. The parents of our houseguests wished to congratulate Max upon his miraculous recovery.

"I told you Max is becoming a celebrity!" my husband laughed. "I even have a 'welcome-home' present for him from one of my patients."

"What is it?"

"A case of dog food. My patient works at a supermarket, so he brought me a whole case of specially nutritious dog food for Maxie!"

"How sweet of him!"

Everybody seemed to be delighted with Max's deliverance. Our neighbors, our mailman, our gardener—they all wanted to know how Maxie pulled through such a terrible ordeal.

Hildy greeted Max with gentle curiosity. She licked his nose, but then, as if understanding that he wasn't well, she stayed at a distance.

Maxie recognized the house at once. He limped on three legs from room to room, sniffing at the furniture and sleeping in the library on his favorite spot on the rug. Hildy respectfully stayed out of his way.

"Isn't it amazing that this frisky, lively puppy understands that her mate is unable to play with her? She actually acts as if she knows what's going on."

"Maybe she does. Who knows what goes on between the animals? There must be something instinctive that allows them to communicate with one another."

*   *   *   *

Maxie's recovery was very swift. Given plenty of highly nourishing food and vitamins and all the love and attention from us and everyone who had ever known him, one could actually see the progress of his recovery from one day to another.

"It's as if we have witnessed a miracle right before our eyes," George said to me. "You know how people always look for some miracle to happen, to see someone win against incredible odds. Well, we have witnessed such a miracle. Anyone who has seen Maxie right after he was found and can see him now would have to agree that it's a miracle he has survived!"

"And lived, to tell his story!" I exclaimed as we all laughed.

As I am writing this, months after he was found, his bandages and splints have been removed, his hair has grown back, his sores have healed, and he has regained his weight.

He is sleek and handsome as he ever was. However, his right hip looks atrophied, and his right hind leg is shorter than the other by about one and one-half inches. It still hangs down, but it is not completely lifeless, although he has no feeling in his foot. Occasionally, as he tries to put his weight on the injured leg, his foot turns under him, and he hops around lopsidedly on all fours, walking on his knuckles, but feeling no pain. Thus, we are encountering a new problem—the danger of having the sores on Maxie's knuckles become infected.

"Do you suppose we could have some kind of a shoe—a boot—designed for him?" George speculated. "There are firms that specialize in orthopedic shoes for all kinds of deformities in people. Perhaps they can create something for Maxie, too."

"It's worth trying," I agreed. "What he needs is some kind of a contraption that will keep his foot from turning under him—something tough and rigid that he won't be able to chew off."

"See if you can find such a company," George suggested. "Give them a call."

I armed myself with several regional telephone books and began leafing through them in search of a suitable orthopedic appliance company. I called them one by one, explaining the situation.

Most of them refused me flatly. "No, we can't make a shoe for a dog," they kept saying. Some of them laughed at my request. "An orthopedic shoe for a dog? You must be kidding!" One or two companies acted as if they were insulted—"We make shoes for people, not for dogs."

I was growing impatient. "What's so strange about making an orthopedic boot for a dog?" I thought as I dialed yet another company.

The man on the other end of the line did not laugh at me, nor did he act insulted.

"We have never made a boot for a dog, but I bet that it can be done. How large is your dog?"

"He's large. He's a Doberman."

The man whistled. "A Doberman? Well, I don't know then. They are vicious."

"Not our dog," I said. "I can bet you a million dollars that Maxie will never hurt you."

The man laughed. "Well, if you bet me a million dollars, then he must be OK! Bring him in. Let me take a look at him."

That evening I took Maxie to the Orthopedic Appliance Company in Hollywood, where George already was waiting for us. This company specialized in various orthopedic appliances—corsets, braces, shoes, artificial limbs, and other prostheses.

"We have never worked on dogs' boots, but I see no reason why we can't try," a young black man, Don Matthews, the designer of shoes, told us. "But I'll have to make a plaster cast of his foot first. Will he bite?"

"Oh, no, Maxie is as gentle as a kitten," George said.

"I still don't trust him," the young man insisted. "You'd better hold his muzzle."

We knelt on the floor next to the dog, and George put his hand over Maxie's long nose. As if understanding that once again someone was going to examine his injured leg,

Maxie stretched it out obligingly toward the young man. We all laughed.

"You see, I told you he was gentle," my husband said.

The young technician stretched a cotton sock over Maxie's foot, then wrapped it with a special bandage covered with a quick-drying plaster of paris. In a few minutes, Maxie's foot was encased in a thick, hard cast. He looked at it with alarm but, seeing us kneeling next to him, he relaxed. He knew that as long as we were there with him, no more harm would come his way.

The technician began to remove the cast with a sharp knife, Max watching him with interest. The young man's dark, handsome face was covered with drops of sweat as he worked over the cast, hurrying to remove it before it would begin to press on Maxie's still not quite healed sores.

"That's a good boy!" Don kept saying reassuringly to Maxie, finally venturing to pat him on the head. Max nuzzled him gratefully.

"I told you that he wouldn't hurt you," my husband smiled.

"Yeah, he sure is nice. I've never seen such a gentle Doberman," the young technician agreed. "But I bet he can be vicious if he has a mind to be."

"Only if we order him to," I said. "He is very well trained."

"OK," the young man said, taking the cast off and standing up. "Call me in a couple of days and we'll have a fitting. I don't know yet what kind of a boot I'll design, but I'll think of something."

"Thank you—see you soon." We left, leading Maxie on leash.

Don stood in the doorway watching Max walk. Undoubtedly he already was figuring out how he was going to proceed with the boot, noticing the need for a special lift to equalize the length of Max's hind legs.

*　　*　　*　　*

side view   front view

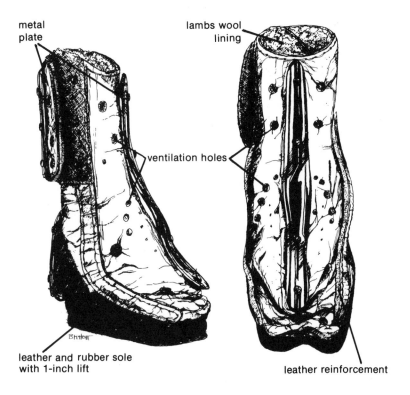

metal plate

lambs wool lining

ventilation holes

leather and rubber sole
with 1-inch lift

leather reinforcement

Max's Orthopedic Boot

Meanwhile, our young Mexican guests, Carlos and Francisco, finally had to go home. School was about to start, and their parents were missing them a lot. It had been a long, lonesome summer for them without their boys. We took the children to the airport, and Carlos at once assumed the responsibility for his younger brother. He personally checked in their luggage, selected their seats on the huge aircraft, and informed the uniformed attendant that instead of the advertised champagne, they would appreciate an extra soft drink.

We hugged and kissed our departing visitors, being genuinely grateful to them for their help with Maxie. As anyone who ever has had to take care of a very sick animal would know, it was not an easy task. Yet, the boys willingly helped us to clean up after the dogs, to feed them both, and to change Maxie's bandages. Saving Maxie's life had become their goal as much as ours.

Now they were leaving. We felt sad, but we knew that they were carrying away with them memories that would stay with them forever. Not only were they speaking more fluent English—the main reason for their spending the summer with us—but they had had the unforgettable experiences of witnessing a valiant creature fighting for his survival, of observing so many fine people combining their various knowledge and skills to save the life of one of God's creatures, and of being a part of this combined effort.

The boys left, promising to keep in touch, making us swear that we would write to them "at least once a week" about Maxie's progress and keep sending his pictures.

"Especially wearing his shoe!" shouted Francisco as he disappeared inside the gleaming airliner.

We returned to the car where the dogs were waiting for us behind their grill. "It's going to be lonely without the kids," George said as if reading my mind.

"Yes, I grew accustomed to their faces—to paraphrase the song," I agreed. "Perhaps we can invite them again for next summer."

"Perhaps."

*   *   *   *

Soon after the departure of our Mexican friends, Hildy came into heat. Since we did not want her to mate with Maxie—she was still too young to have puppies and Maxie was not yet completely recovered to make a good sire—we decided to keep the dogs separated from one another as much as possible.

It was easier said than done. It was reasonably simple during the night—we just locked them up in different parts of the house. But during the day it was almost impossible to keep them apart. Hildy was still manageable, but Maxie! Obviously he had forgotten about his infirmities, remembering only the pleasures of courtship.

Hildy and Max carried on like two spoiled children, whimpering, crying to be together, scratching at the doors, and chewing on the door frames like puppies. If allowed to continue in that crazy way, they would have torn our house apart. Obviously, something had to be done.

George decided to take Maxie to the office with him during the day. He had a suite of rooms there, including a tiny kitchenette where Max could stay while George was with his patients.

The first day was a success. Maxie behaved like the well-bred dog that he was, making no noise, no mess, going for a walk with George during his lunch hour, then for another walk with George's secretary.

Encouraged, George took Max to the office the next day. And this is how our Max became the "canine psychiatric aide" to my husband.

At first one patient, then another, then several more, began to express their interest in Max. They all noticed his disfigured hip and shortened leg, and the dog's infirmity apparently struck some sympathetic chord in their minds and unlocked some doors that they previously had kept locked to guard against all intruders, including their physicians. Watching Maxie hobble around, his aristocratic, long, narrow head held high and proud as ever, the patients began to talk about him. Eventually they began to talk about themselves and about their own deep-seated feelings of physical infirmity, something that they previously had been resistant to doing.

One specific incident in which Maxie was the key that unlocked the doors to a tormented soul stands out in my mind as described to me by George.

"I have a patient, a middle-aged black woman who was referred to me by Local 777—the Retail Clerk's Union. She worked as a checker at one of the supermarkets and, according to the manager, was suffering from uncontrollable spells of hysterical weeping that would strike her at odd times.

"No amount of talking and reasoning from her well-meaning fellow employees seemed to help, so she was referred to me.

"Melba was a widow, rather good-looking, who was living alone. Her two grown sons were long gone from home, one in the army, another she knew not where. She was very cooperative in talking about her life, which seemed to be well organized between her work and her church. But each time that I tried to find out what made her cry, she would clam up and burst into tears. Obviously at the core of her depression was something that she could not bring herself to talk about—some deep secret."

"Perhaps it was her missing son," I suggested.

"Thank you, Ms. Psychiatrist," George replied sarcastically. "Of course I thought of it. But Melba made peace long ago with the fact that her missing son was 'no good.' Her other son, a sergeant in the army, was her pride and joy. He was attentive to her and was contemplating marriage to a nice girl of whom she highly approved. No, that wasn't it."

"Money?"

"No. She made good wages, had some savings, and she owned her home—free and clear."

"Loneliness?"

"Aha, you're getting warm. Yes, I suspected that it was loneliness, yet she told me that she had many friends, was very active in her church, and worked as a volunteer once a week at the children's hospital. No, her loneliness was of a different kind."

"Love? Or rather the absence of it?"

"She had a devoted friend who, according to her, wished to marry her."

"But?"

"But she preferred her independence. She had a generally low opinion of men. She was making more money than he did, and she felt that he was one of those happy-go-lucky charmers who would allow her to work for his support. She enjoyed his company, but she didn't trust him. I found her very intelligent and easy to talk to, except when it came to her tears. She would start sniffling as the torrents of uncontrolled tears silently rolled down her cheeks. There would be no further use talking to her that day."

"Could you do anything for her?"

"Sure. I gave her certain medications to help her emerge from her depression. But it is often of great help to patients to explore all the possible reasons for their depression so that they can express their feelings in a more specific way."

"I understand."

"So, try as I may, I was unable to penetrate her wall of tears. At this point, Maxie appeared. Without even trying, he solved all the problems!"

"Really?"

"Yes. I'm being facetious, of course, but one morning when I had my session with Melba, Maxie scratched at the door in my kitchenette. 'What's that?' Melba asked in surprise. 'Oh, it's my dog.' I explained briefly why I had to bring Maxie to my office. She listened attentively. 'May I see him?' she suddenly asked. 'Sure,' I said and opened the door.

"Maxie entered the room and paused at the doorway. Then he hobbled straight to Melba and placed his head on her lap. Melba burst out in loud lamentations, tears just streaming down her face. She petted Maxie's head, not a bit afraid of him.

"What about Maxie?"

"He loved it! You know how he loves to be petted—as if he never could have enough of it. And you know how fast his tongue is when he tries to lick you. Not for nothing do I call him 'the fastest tongue in the West!' He loved it! He licked Melba's tear-stricken face, while Melba petted him all over, mumbling through her sobs, 'You, my poor black boy.' This scene continued for a good five minutes, if not longer, both Melba and Maxie revelling in it for different reasons. As I watched Melba, I suddenly noticed that there was a difference in her tears. While before her tears had always been silent, now her nose was running, and she was sobbing and mumbling, sighing deeply and wailing like an old woman at an Irish wake."

"It couldn't be on account of Maxie's ordeal!" I exclaimed with conviction.

"Of course not. But seeing Max and his behavior toward her obviously made Melba associate it with something else—perhaps her own private grief or, most likely, the cause of her depressive episode."

"So what happened?"

"Well, I let her carry on until Maxie got bored by it and climbed on my couch for a nap. Then I gave Melba a box of tissue and said, 'Tell me about it.' "

"And she did?"

"Yes, she did. Little by little she told me the familiar story of the loss of a beloved creature and of her mourning for this creature. She told me that she had had to put her poodle to sleep because of old age and a bunch of incurable canine diseases. She told me about the agony that she had gone through while making this decision—the four trips that she had made to her vet only to change her mind at the last moment and return home with her sick dog. She described how, unable to watch him suffer, yet unable to take him to his death as well, she paid her neighbor to take the dog on his final trip."

"Poor lady. You and I surely know how she must have felt!" I said sympathetically.

"Yes. You and I and thousands of other animal lovers," George agreed. "Anyway, she was mourning the death of her beloved poodle, unable to sleep, crying without stopping. She took a few days off from work, hoping to recover from her grief, but everything reminded her of her dog. If there was a dog on a television commercial, she cried. If she saw a dog walking along with his master, she cried. Even when

she heard a distant bark of a dog, she cried. Yet she was ashamed to admit to anyone the intensity of her grief. She bottled it up within herself, unable to share it with her friends. It became so bad that she cried even while at work. She told me that it had happened quite unexpectedly. She had been checking out someone's groceries when she had come upon a twenty-five-pound bag of dog food, the type she used to buy for her poodle. She had been unable to continue her work. She had burst out in tears and had had to run to the ladies' room!"

"Poor Melba!"

"Yes. It happened to her several more times, and with all kinds of dog food, not only her dog's favorite. Finally, the manager decided that something had to be done about her crying. It was upsetting the customers, not to mention the clerks in the store. He tried to talk to Melba, but she would not disclose the reason for her grief. Of course, no one connected her tears with the dog food. It was her own secret, shameful and laughable, as she thought. Anyway, that was the time when the union physician recommended that she come to see me."

"So, what happened next?"

"Well, after Melba had unburdened herself to me and saw that not only did I not ridicule nor scold her for her deep feelings for a dog, but rather shared with her my own grief when I thought that Maxie was gone forever, she was able to face her problem in a constructive and realistic way. I continued to prescribe for her a mild antidepressant, and she continued to see me for psychotherapy. But the last time I saw her, she was like a new person. She realized that she need never forget her poodle, but she was now able to cope with her loss. She came to recognize how the loss of her adored pet was connected with the other painful losses of her life—her husband, her 'no-good son,' whom she missed in spite of her denials. She began to deal realistically with her life."

"And you have not seen her since?"

"As a patient—no. But not long ago she came to see me as a friend. She came to show me her new puppy, a Yorkie, whom she had named Maxie."

"What a wonderful ending!" I exclaimed.

"Yes. Thanks to our Max, Melba was relieved of her terrible burden. Who knows how long she might have continued to suffer in silence were it not for Maxie, who licked her tears away!"

"Literally and symbolically!" I added.

To be sure, not all of the patients reacted to Maxie's presence with such beneficial results. Some were afraid of him, and many were indifferent, but those who liked him and learned about his ordeal began to "open up" more rapidly than before.

When at last Maxie appeared at the office wearing his new orthopedic shoe with an inch-high lift, the patients cheered. Many began to identify with Max, feeling that his tenacious will to survive and to recover his health inspired their own struggle against their illness. If a mere dog could survive and win against such odds, surely they, thinking intelligent men and women, could do it, too! Perhaps some of them had a new insight toward my husband. These patients saw my husband for the first time not only as their psychiatrist, but as a kind, compassionate man. They observed the relationship between George and Maxie, and they felt the currents of love passing between the man and his dog. The patients felt that they could trust this man, who was so kind to a mere dog. They instinctively began to seek the touch of his hand, to watch for a smile on his face, to show them that he was pleased with them. They began to trust him. They began to open up, expecting him to heal them, to make them feel better.

"You ought to write about Maxie's therapeutic effects on your patients for one of your medical journals!" I suggested jokingly to George. "Perhaps you have a psychiatric 'breakthrough' on your hands and don't know it!"

George smiled and patted Maxie's head. "I agree," he said. "Someone should write about Maxie's trials and triumphs. I think you should do it. You're the published author in our family."

Maxie looked up at me and gave me his paw without being asked to.

"See? He approves of the idea!" George laughed.

Maxie barked happily as I shook his paw.

"Okay, Maxie, you deserve a book written about you," I said. "I'll be your biographer."

Max listened, cocking his head a little as was his habit when he did not quite understand what he was to do. Not recognizing any familiar words, he climbed up on the sofa and sighed deeply, ready for a nap.

He couldn't care less whether anyone was going to write his biography.

Two Years Later

Two years have gone by since Maxie's ordeal in Sequoia National Forest.

It took that long for all of his injuries and ulcerations to heal, but heal they finally did. Although his right hind leg is shorter now, he manages to use it most of the time. Only when he is very tired does he allow it to hang helplessly while hobbling around on three legs.

Maxie seldom needs his orthopedic shoe. However, when we take him for a run in a rough terrain, we do put his boot on to protect his foot. He still has a metal plate in his hip, but it does not bother him. He chases around the house with Hildy even though he is rather clumsy and Hildy takes advantage of him. She often knocks him off his feet, and I have the feeling that Maxie is embarrassed by his inability to stand up to her. She has become the boss. But, of course, I keep attributing human emotions to the dog. Max knows how to deal with her. When he has had enough of her aggressiveness, he just picks himself up and climbs on his favorite sofa. Hildy knows then that the game is over. She climbs on the sofa, too, and with contented sighs they both go to sleep. They cuddle up cozily, with the head of one resting on the back of another, as they used to do when they were puppies.

We never bred them. I am sorry that we will never have puppies from Maxie and Hildy, but we were advised by the veterinarian to have Hildy spayed early during Maxie's recuperation. His injuries required daily care and bandaging of his legs, and the dogs in the throes of their biological needs were practically unmanageable. To save Max from further injuries, we agreed to have Hildy spayed. Interestingly enough, Maxie's personality changed. While before his accident he was an alert and obedient guard dog, Max now has become a rather lazy and stubborn sybarite. He allows Hildy to do all the barking and threatening and showing of fangs. He joins her only when he deems it absolutely necessary. While Hildy distrusts and dislikes strangers, Max now loves everyone. Apparently his experience during long months of recovery, when so many strangers handled his injured body so tenderly, made him trustful of all people.

He loves everybody. He licks people's faces at the first opportunity, which is quite embarrasing to us because not everyone likes to be licked by a huge Doberman.

But Max is a charmer. He smiles at people, gives them his paw, and only a rare person can resist him. Besides, most of our friends know about his misfortune and are sympathetic.

Max couldn't ask for anything better. He usually makes rounds from one person to another, sticking his head under people's hands, urging them to stroke him. If he feels that the person doesn't do a good job at petting him, Max nudges persistently, always managing to get a few more strokes. Happy beyond measure, he begins to utter little sighs of contentment that sound almost like the purring of a cat. Inevitably, it makes people laugh as they increase their stroking of Maxie's satiny skin. Maxie then all but dissolves in total happiness.

George occasionally takes him to his office, but now that Max doesn't wear any bandages nor his orthopedic shoe, the patients fail to notice his infirmity. To them Max is a large dog with the bad reputation of a Doberman. They are wary of him, and only the animal lovers among them and children from the children's ward are aware of his gentleness. The others stay out of his way, not able to identify with him any more.

The author Kyra Wayne and Max. Note Max's orthopedic shoe.

Thus, Maxie's career as a "canine psychiatric aide" has come to an end. But George and I are content with the results. Max has triumphantly survived his ordeal. He continues to give us pleasure, for he has become more than a dog to us. He has become a symbol, an inspiration. His valiant fight for his life, the devotion that he inspired in so many people who had struggled for his recovery, truly makes one believe in the basic goodness of all creatures and once again reaffirms the value of life.

Any life.

Even the life of a dog.

Epilogue

Ever since this book was published in 1979, my editors and I have received hundreds of letters from readers who wanted to know whether Max was still alive or what had happened to our young Mexican friends Carlos and Francisco.

Briefly, I'll bring the story up to date.

Carlos is now a doctor and has been involved in the research and treatment of AIDS and other contagious diseases. He and his wife, also a doctor, have two children—Vicente and Victoria. Recently Carlos and his family moved to Atlanta, Georgia where Carlos is engaged in important medical research.

Francisco is a lawyer. His wife is an architect and they also have two children—Lorenza and Carlos. The children are learning to read English so soon they'll be able to read about Max by themselves, although they have heard the story about his adventures from their parents. The story of Max is one of their favorites.

Our own son, Ron, is also a doctor, an anesthesiologist. He has five kids, the eldest of whom, Nicky, used to help me bandage Max's atrophied leg.

As for Max himself—he's long gone.

*   *   *   *

Max was almost fourteen years old, deaf and blind, when during a routine check-up a veterinarian had discovered tumors in his lungs and liver. The tumors proved to be malignant.

My husband and I realized that we had to make an important decision: either to wait for Max to die a natural death or to "put him to sleep", as the euphemism goes.

"How long do you think he may have?" George asked the doctor.

"Hard to say. Not long. His main organs are affected. A couple of weeks... Perhaps, a month. I strongly recommend euthanasia."

"Put him to sleep," George said softly, caressing Max's head.

"Yes. You wouldn't want him to suffer. He's in pain already. It will only be getting worse."

"Is there a way to ease the pain?" I asked. "Perhaps we can still keep him alive for a while."

"Sure, there are medications. But he doesn't enjoy life anymore. He's blind, he can't hear and, as you say, he has stopped eating. He's not going to get any better. His cancer is terminal. It's the only humane thing to do—put him to sleep. Don't prolong his suffering."

George and I knew that the doctor was right. Our beloved Max came to the end of his life.

"We'll give him a shot and he'll go to sleep. He won't feel anything," the doctor continued. "At fourteen he has already outlived his normal life expectancy. Every year of a dog's life roughly equals seven years of human life. And the first year usually counts for twice as many. At fourteen Max has reached about ninety- eight years of human life."

"Ninety-eight years old if he were a man," George repeated. "Almost a century old!"

"Yes. He has lived a happy life," the doctor said. "Don't let him die in agony. His time has come. Let him go."

Max was stretched out on a metal examining table, breathing with difficulty. His tongue was hanging out of his mouth as if it were a piece of red flannel. His breath came out in shallow short bursts. His bony ribcage trembled as he inhaled and seem to collapse as he exhaled. His sightless eyes, clouded with whitish film, were wide open, but he saw nothing. His body, once so sleek, looked emaciated, almost as thin and bony as it had looked when we brought him home after his accident in the Sierras so many years ago.

Softly, George said, "We must do it."

I began to cry. "Wait...wait... Perhaps something still can be done...What if the X-rays were not conclusive?"

The doctor shook his head. "They're conclusive. Besides, there are the results of blood tests. They're all positive. No, my dear lady, your Max has no chance of recovery. He'll only get worse. I strongly recommend putting him to sleep. Today. Now. You don't want to prolong his painful condition."

"So be it," George said, his own eyes misting.

I kissed Max on his forehead and George ran his hand over his thin body in a last caress.

"Good bye, old friend," I whispered, choking on my tears. Max could not hear me.

We left the animal hospital. Our valiant Max, the dog that refused to die, has finally lost his battle.

* * * *

Hildy, our other Doberman, searched for Max. She went from room to room in the house, from shrub to shrub in the garden searching for her companion. She couldn't understand why her friend, with whom she had shared her life, why was he suddenly not there. She sniffed around the basket where he had slept, but did not try to take it over as she had done before, Max always chasing her out. This time, she just sniffed, circling the empty basket, waiting for Max to return. She finally stretched down next to it, looking forlorn, her graying narrow muzzle resting on her crossed front paws.

"She, too, is getting old," I thought.

"She's missing Max," I told George that night. "She keeps vigil at his basket."

"I'll take it to the garage," George said. "Looking at his basket makes me sad too. With Max gone, the house feels empty."

"It's amazing how gloomy our lives have become," I thought. "Even though Max was old and sick and spent most of his days dozing, his presence was felt by all of us—George, me and Hildy. With Max gone—there's a vacuum, an empty space..." It was almost as bad as when our son, Ron, went away to college. Then, too, we felt that emptiness in the house. But then it was the natural progression of life, when the young leave the family to start their own lives and careers. Our Ron became a doctor, like his father, has married and acquired a family of his own. It was a happy progression and the vacuum created by his leaving our home was eventually filled by a new daughter-in-law and the children.

The emptiness created by Max's death remained an emptiness.

* * * *

I decided to act. I knew that the best and the quickest way of getting out of the hole of depression over Max's death was to get a new puppy. He would not let us grieve. He would demand our attention. He would cheer us up and he would shake Hildy out of her apathy as well.

I started browsing through the classified sections of The Los Angeles Times. I wanted to get a different breed of dog this time, something smaller, less powerful than a Doberman. The rigors of training a large dog were beyond us now . George and I were getting old. We needed to simplify our lives. We planned to move out of Los Angeles to some smaller and quieter place as soon as George would retire from practice. Big dogs were out of the question now.

We bought a Yorkshire Terrier, a tiny ball of soft fur, shiny black nose and bright eyes, a little package of joy, weighing no more than four pounds. We named him Max.

Maxie rejuvenated Hildy. The mischievous puppy ran her ragged, stealing a few morsels of her food right from under her nose. He paid no attention to her warning growls, knowing instinctively that no grown dog would ever hurt a puppy. Hildy soon learned that Maxie's small mouth couldn't manage the large chunks of her kibble. She stopped guarding her food and just watched the spunky little guy with amusement as he would struggle with a stolen chunk, too big for him. Finally, Maxie would give up and retreat under the chair from where he would growl at Hildy as she crunched the pieces that he had to abandon. The game continued every day at feeding time, both dogs obviously enjoying the ritual.

Sometimes, Max would entice Hildy for a game of chase. He would stand in front of her basket and bark, shrilly and urgently, until she would give up her cozy nest. Pretending to be ferocious, she would charge at him, but Maxie, fast as lightning, would dash under a chair. He would bark at her from his sanctuary, as if teasing, knowing that she couldn't reach him.

Hildy had a trick of her own. She would pretend that she had no interest in Maxie. Stretching lazily, yawning, she would lie down near his hiding place, waiting for his puppy curiosity to make him abandon his hiding place. Then she would pounce on him.

But Maxie was much too fast for her. He would dive under the chair again and yap triumphantly. He had fooled her again!

We laughed as we watched their game of "hide-and-bark", and the dogs, realizing that we enjoyed it, never failed to put on the best show.

Then, a third dog joined our family.

FEATHER

One day, a friend of ours, Mrs. Fomenko, who owned a small jewelry store, telephoned me. "I have a problem," she began. "Perhaps you can help me."

"What kind of a problem?"

"I found a lost dog a week ago. Or, rather, this dog found me," she corrected herself with a chuckle." I was walking to my car across the parking lot at our market when I saw this little itsy-bitsy dog being chased by a couple of kids. The dog looked terrified..." she paused. "She's a cute little thing. Friendly, too. She's on my lap now."

"What kind of dog is she?"

"I don't quite know. She's beautiful, fluffy. Sort of, like your Maxie. She has a soft silvery coat. And a beautiful little face. Anyway, " Mrs. Fomenko continued, "I was just about to scold the kids for chasing the dog, when the dog jumped right into my arms. She actually jumped ! It's beyond belief how such a tiny creature could've jumped so high, right into a person's arms, but she did! She was trembling all over. I asked the kids whether it was their dog or if they knew whom she belonged to, but they said no. So, I took this frightened creature home with me, thinking that I'll try to find her owners. She was obviously an expensive dog. Well trained. House-broken."

"Does she have any tags?"

"No. No tags, no collar. Nothing."

"Then how will you find her owners?"

"My husband and I advertised in our local paper. We gave the name of the market parking lot where I had found her and we included our telephone number."

"Any luck?"

"No. Several people responded to our ad but none of them could give us the correct description that would fit the little dog.

Obviously their lost dogs were not the one that I have in my spare room."

"Why don't you keep her yourselves? You love animals."

"Yes, we love animals, and just because of that, we can't keep her. You see, our old tom cat can't stand her. He's unhappy that she's in the house. He's a jealous sort. He's twice her size and by nature, he's very aggressive. He attacks her even in our presence, and I shudder to think of what he might do to her when we're not around! Besides, dogs require different care than cats. It's not fair to keep a dog locked up all day while we're away at our store. No, I must find her a good home. Do you know of anyone who might take her in?"

"Yes. Me."

"But you have two dogs already!"

"One more will make no difference. Especially, a small dog."

"Do you really mean it? You want her?"

"Yes. I do."

"Well, in that case, I'll bring her to our store tomorrow. Perhaps you can come and take a look at her. But if you change your mind..."

"I won't change my mind. George and I will be happy to adopt your little foundling."

"Wonderful! I couldn't have hoped for anything better!"

"See you tomorrow. What's her name?"

"I have no idea. As I've said, she had no tags."

"No matter. We'll give her a name. See you tomorrow."

"Are you sure that we need another dog? I thought we had agreed to simplify our lives." George shook his head.

"One small dog won't complicate our lives. She'll be a companion for Maxie. As you know, Hildy is getting old. She doesn't like to be bothered by Maxie. She's becoming very cantankerous. Maxie needs a playmate."

"True. Well, go and see this little dog. If you like her..."

"Yes! I'll bring her home." I kissed George. "I promise, I'll follow my own 'gut' feeling about the dog. If my 'gut' says 'no,' I'll say 'no' to Mrs. Fomenko."

"I'm sure your 'gut' will say 'yes' I know you," George laughed.

Of course, George was right. The moment I saw the little creature, I fell in love with her. She was a little bigger than Maxie and her coloring was different—golden on her head and silvery on the rest of her body, while Maxie's colors were basically black and tan. But her long soft hair was just as fine and silky to touch and her dark eyes and nose were three little buttons peering from under the hair.

"I think, she's a Silky, not a Yorkie," I said. "I really don't know the difference, but I do recall seeing Silkies at a dog show. She looks just like them."

"Do you like her?" There was concern in Mrs. Fomenko's voice.

"Yes, I do. I like her very much. If you still don't want to keep her, I'll take her."

"Good! I'm glad that you haven't changed your mind. I was afraid that the good doctor might not want to have another dog."

"My husband is just as crazy about the animals as I am. He left the decision to my 'gut' feeling," I laughed.

"Then it's settled! Take the dog. Let me know how she'll be getting along with your dogs, OK?"

"OK! Thanks. I'll call you in a couple of days." We placed the dog into a portable carrier and I kissed Mrs. Fomenko good-bye.

* * * *

The dog cried and yelped and barked in the carrier as I drove. I tried to play some music on my radio to drown the noise, but she kept crying and yelping and barking even louder. Finally, I pulled to the curb and stopped the car.

"What's the matter, baby?" I said as I opened the little door of the carrier. The dog promptly jumped out and climbed on my lap.

"Ah, that's what you want!" I started the car. The dog shifted on my knees to a more comfortable position, gave a deep sigh of contentment and went to sleep, the tip of her pink tongue sticking out as if she were a cat.

"I'm accepted," I thought.

* * * *

Waiting for my husband to come home from the office I introduced the new dog to Maxie and Hildy. Maxie sniffed her and gave a tentative bark, inviting her to play, but she was too shy. She stayed near me, walking behind me from room to room, climbing on my lap whenever I sat down.

Maxie didn't like it. It was his prerogative to sit on my lap! He tried to claim his right, but the newcomer growled at him menacingly and showed her teeth, or rather, her gums, for her front teeth were missing. She looked like the kid in the popular Christmas song "All I Want For Christmas Is My Two Front Teeth". No wonder her tongue was falling out of her mouth! She had no front teeth to keep it in. Fortunately, her other teeth were intact, the sharp canines looking shiny and strong.

"Are you an old doggy?"

She looked at me, trying to understand what was wrong. My voice must've sounded as if I were disapproving of her. She licked my hand.

"Don't worry, little one, toothless or not, young or old, I already love you. You're one of us," I said patting her shiny little head, no bigger than my fist.

* * * *

I met George at the door, holding the new dog in my arms.

"Well, here she is, our new baby."

"She's cute. Have you named her?"

"Not yet. I'll leave it up to you. I named Maxie, so it's your turn."

George petted the dog. "She's so soft... Soft like a feather. That's it! Let's name her Feather!"

"I like it. Tomorrow I'll buy her a collar and a tag with her name on it. And, our telephone number. I don't want her to get lost again."

Feather snuggled in George's arms feeling secure, knowing that she'd be loved and cherished from now on.

"What about Maxie? Did he accept her?"

"Oh, he'll get used to her. She rebuffed him, but he's still a puppy. He's not easily insulted. They'll be friends."

"And Hildy?"

"So far, she pretends that Feather doesn't exist. But Hildy is not given to friendships. As you know, she loved big Max and ever since he has died, she doesn't like anyone, except you and me. She's very moody."

"She's old," George said. "She's almost twelve. We must pay special attention to her. She should never feel neglected."

"She will never be neglected. But, do you know, I think Feather is also old. Did you notice, she has no front teeth!"

"Really? Well, it doesn't matter. Perhaps we can outfit her with a set of false teeth," George joked. " Remember how we ordered an orthopedic shoe for Max? Everyone laughed at us but it served him for more than ten years. I like Feather. Toothless or not - I like her. She's sweet."

"I'm so glad. I like her too."

* * * *

Maxie and Feather soon became inseparable. As the weather turned cold they often shared their padded bed, cuddling together in a ball of soft fur.

Meanwhile, Hildy, like so many large dogs, began to show the signs of hip dysplasia. Her hind legs had weakened considerably and she had difficulty in walking. She preferred to stay in her basket, getting up with effort only when called to eat. She became incontinent, unable to control her bladder. She whimpered in pain when we carried her out to relieve herself. Sometimes she collapsed, her hind legs splaying flat on the grass.

"She's dying," George said. "Her time, too, has come."

Once again, we made the sad journey to the animal hospital. Once again, the veterinarian pronounced the verdict: Hildy has reached the point of no hope. Once again, we bid our friend good-bye.

"Thank God for Maxie and Feather," George said softly as we drove home.

"Yes," I thought. "Maxie and Feather will make it easier to accept the loss of Hildy."

"How unfair it is that the dogs have such a short span of life," George continued. "Ten or twelve or even fifteen years is not enough. Just look how many wonderful dogs we've lost in our own lifetime ! Our two Weimaraners, Tony and Lori, our beautiful foundling Milah, the Shepherd, then, the big Max, and now - Hildy! All gone."

"But we still have the little ones. Maxie and Feather!"

"Yes, thank God for them."

We drove the rest of the way in silence, Hildy's empty dog bed sliding back and forth behind us in the cargo section of our station wagon.

Hildy was no more.

* * * *

A couple of years passed in relative tranquillity. I worked on a novel about Alaska at the time when it belonged to Russia. George continued his work as a Medical Director of a hospital and teaching at UCLA.

Then, a calamity struck us. George developed a serious heart condition that required open heart surgery.

"Can't you do something 'magical' for me?" George tried to joke. "You're so good saving dogs, why can't you do something for me, the good old dog that I am?"

"I wish I could," I shook my head. "But you'll pull through, I know. Think of Max and his fight for his life. Let him be your inspiration."

"Yes," he said without much conviction.

I drove him to the hospital.

* * * *

After George recuperated from the surgery, we decided that the time had come for him to retire and for us to leave the busy and crowded city of Los Angeles for some quieter place.

We chose to move to the Monterey peninsula where the summers were cool and the winters mild, the springs and the autumns—glorious. We built our "dream house" on the top of a hill, overlooking the mountains in one direction and Monterey Bay in the other. We surrounded the house and the garden with a tall fence to keep our little dogs safe from the coyotes and mountain lions that inhabited the canyons around us.

But something was still missing.

"We need a big dog," George announced one day. "Our Maxie and Feather are toys. Cute and lovely, but they're toys.. We must have a real dog! I miss a real bark!"

"What kind of a dog?" I thought that I already knew the answer.

"A Doberman."

"I thought so." I sighed. I knew that it would be my responsibility to take care of the dog and to train him. George was becoming too ill. He couldn't take care of a large dog.

"Don't you want another Dobie?" George looked at me, almost pleadingly.

"Sure!" I wanted to please my ailing husband whenever I could. If he wanted a Doberman-he should have one. If he wanted a horse-I would've gotten one, too. "Let's look at some ads in the paper," I said.

"I've already looked and I found two or three possibilities," George said sheepishly. "Here. It may be exactly what we want."

One advertisement described a chocolate-brown male Doberman, seven-months old, housebroken and with ears already cropped.

"It looks like what we might want... Housebroken and with ears cropped. The worst part of raising a Doberman puppy is already done. How about it?"

"Well, sounds good. Call them up. Let them bring the dog here so that we can see how he behaves toward the little ones. I don't want a mean Doberman"

"Neither do I" George picked up the telephone.

PEPPER

A tall husky man and a young skinny girl wearing a huge denim jacket, obviously not her own, drove into our yard. The man parked his van under a tree and opened the side door. A large Doberman, still awkward, but showing the signs of eventually becoming a powerful animal, jumped out.

"He's a handsome brute," George murmured. "I like what I see."

"What's his name?" I asked the girl.

"Pepper. His proper registered name is Red Pepper of Soquel," she replied catching the dog by the collar. "His daddy is a champion, and so is his granddaddy," she added with pride.

"Why do you want to sell him?"

"Because this year we've raised too many dogs," the man said. "We have three more puppies for sale. Do you want to see them? They are in the cages in the back of the van. They are younger, though, and they still need to have their ears cropped."

"I'd rather not go through that again," I thought as I patted Pepper's smooth head. But the puppies! How can one resist seeing puppies!

They were adorable black and tan creatures reminding me of our big Max and they yapped shrilly when they saw us.

"They are three months old, from the same litter," the man said. "They're cheaper than Pepper, but you've said that you wanted an older dog."

"Yes, we do want an older dog," I said quickly, afraid that George might succumb to the charm of the irresistible puppies. "I like Pepper. I like him very much."

Pepper, hearing his name, moved closer to my leg, almost pushing me against the car. "Boy, you're a strong one," I laughed. Pepper licked my hand, as if thanking me for the compliment.

"I like Pepper too," George declared. "Now, let's see how he behaves toward our little dogs."

We all went into the house, George holding Pepper by the collar.

Maxie and Feather met us at the door with ear-splitting yaps. They had never seen such a big dog. Pepper stood still, his ears slightly twitching as a barely visible tremble ran under his shiny coat.

George laughed. "Are you a coward? Are you afraid of these little mutts?"

"Let him go," I said. "Let's see what he'll do. "George let go of Pepper's collar.

The dog made two tentative steps toward the little dogs.

"Sit!" the man commanded. Pepper obeyed. Maxie and Feather approached him cautiously. Pepper sat motionlessly, only his trembling muscles betraying his concentration. Maxie and Feather circled around him, sniffing at his paws, ready to run under a chair at his first move, but Pepper remained immobile.

I liked that. Pepper was obviously intelligent and obedient.

At last, the little dogs must've decided that Pepper was not posing any threat. Maxie placed himself in front of him and looking up at his face, gave a short, tentative bark, just once.

It must've been something nice in dog language, for Pepper jumped up. Maxie ran to the door, his little tail wagging in a friendly manner, inviting Pepper to follow him. Feather trotted behind, the three of them spilling out into the sunny garden, a trio of healthy and happy pals.

The puppies in the van broke out in a cacophony of shrill barks. They, too, were eager to participate in a game of chase.

"Let them out," I said to the man. He opened the cages and the puppies jumped out.

"I wish I could keep them all," I thought watching the six dogs cavorting in my garden. Pepper towered over them, a gentle giant. The puppies and our dogs showed no fear of him.

"Well, Pepper is our boy!" George decided. "I like what I see. Maxie and Feather also approve of him."

"Pepper is a great pup," the man said pocketing George's check. "He'll be a good friend. And a great watchdog. However, if for some reason you decide not to keep him, give me a call. We'll find you some other dog."

"I think Pepper fits right in. I like him a lot. He's gentle," I said. "But thanks, just the same."

＊　＊　＊　＊

Pepper did fit right in. He was a well-mannered dog who showed his intelligence from the very first day. As he ate his first meal at his new home I watched him closely. Would he protect his food from Maxie who had a bad habit of stealing from Hildy and probably would try to do the same with Pepper?

I saw Maxie cautiously approach Pepper's plate. The big dog raised his head. The little dog dashed forward and quickly grabbed a piece of kibble off the floor near Pepper's plate. He was so fast that the big dog had no time to react. He stood there, dumbfounded, surprised at Maxie's impertinence.

"It's all right," I said patting Pepper's head. "Go ahead and eat." He resumed his eating, glancing suspiciously now and then at Maxie who was struggling with his stolen piece, too large for his tiny mouth.

When Maxie repeated his assault on Pepper's food, the big dog growled a warning. His growl didn't sound threatening. Just a warning, to which Maxie paid no attention. He grabbed another morsel and ran with it under a chair, just like he used to do with Hildy.

Pepper must've decided that the amount of food that Maxie was stealing wasn't worth fighting for. From then on, he allowed Maxie to take a few pieces off his plate. In return, he licked Maxie's dish clean, often even before Maxie was through eating.

"They're even," I declared.

Feather, on the other hand, had established her dominance from the start. She fiercely attacked Pepper when he tried to lick her plate and Pepper, who was at least twenty times her size, retreated, never to try it again.

George and I watched with fascination this play for dominance.

"Do you suppose, Feather, as the eldest of the three, demanded and got Pepper's respect?" I was curious.

"Perhaps. It's amazing how this tiny creature could intimidate a huge hundred-pound beast, such as Pepper. She's feisty!"

"Yes. Maybe it's because she's the female? Pepper behaves toward her as if she were his aging mother. He's never rambunctious with her, while with Maxie, well, you know how he is with Maxie! They play all the time. I just love watching them chase one another in the garden!"

"It would be interesting to research this idea. Do animals have 'respect' for their mothers?" he chuckled. "But you're right. Watching the dogs chase one another in the garden adds life to the placid existence of retirement."

"The placid existence of retirement" lasted only a couple of years. Soon it was shattered forever.

A YEAR OF TROUBLE

First, we almost lost Maxie due to a freak accident. George had been puttering in the garage and wasn't aware that Maxie was dozing in the sunny spot nearby. George had lifted a heavy board but it slipped out of his hands and fell on the sleeping Maxie, knocking him unconscious.

"My God!" George panicked, "I killed Maxie! I killed my Maxie!" he cried running into the house with the lifeless body of our little dog.

Maxie wasn't breathing. His body was limp, his eyes glazed. My strong husband, a doctor , had lost control over his emotions. His face was contorted in pain. "I've killed my Maxie!"

"Get your stethoscope," I commanded as I grabbed the dog from him. I turned Maxie on his back and probed for his heart. There was a faint heartbeat. "He's still alive," I thought. Maxie's little legs, sticking up stiffly, looked like they were the legs of a teddy bear.

I pried his mouth open and began to breathe into it. "Thank God I learned CPR!" I felt his chest move under my fingers as his lungs filled with air.

By the time George returned with his stethoscope, which he couldn't find in his distress, Maxie began to breathe.

"You've saved him! Without CPR, he would've died." George said.

Maxie was breathing on his own. He opened his eyes. They lost their glassy appearance but there was no sparkle in them. When I finally put Maxie on the floor, he fell on his side and lay there, weak and disoriented.

"We must take him to the vet," George said.

We drove to the animal emergency clinic and described to the doctor on duty what had happened to Maxie.

"Well, he's one lucky pup. You've indeed, saved his life," the doctor said probing Maxie's body for possible injuries. "I can't find any broken bones but just the same, leave him here for a couple of days so that we can run a few tests and have some X-rays done."

"Of course."

We left the clinic. A flood of memories about the big Max and his ordeal filled our thoughts The same anxious thoughts tormented us, "Will he survive? Would he be 'normal'?"

"What do you think? Will Maxie pull through?" George said.

"Of course he'll pull through!" I replied brightly, not at all sure that he would.

. . . .

A few days later I brought Maxie back home. He seemed to be different. The joy of life was gone from him. He had no appetite and he stopped barking. He became mute. He stayed in his bed, barely moving, holding his head rigidly high, moving his whole body in response to a call as if he couldn't turn his head.

I probed the taut knotted muscles in his neck. "He feels stiff as a board."

"It is a natural reflex. He protects himself from pain by stiffening his muscles," George explained. "It's like when one has a stiff neck. One tries not to move it, even though one knows that the movement would be beneficial."

"The doctor suggested that I massage his neck. It may relax his throat so he could bark. Apparently he has spasms in his throat and they prevent him from barking."

"By all means, try the massage. It feels weird to have a silent dog".

I picked Maxie up and began the "physical therapy", gently massaging his tiny neck, so tiny that I could encircle it with my two fingers.

Twice a day Maxie submitted to this treatment, remaining mute, holding his head rigidly up.

"He's not responding," I thought in despair "I must make him relax. But how?" I decided to try my own proven method of relaxation. A warm bath. It had never failed to soothe my own hurting back or neck or whatever ailed me. Perhaps, it would work with Maxie. He always seemed to enjoy having a bath. Perhaps, it would work.

I filled a dishpan with soapy warm water and placed Maxie in it. He stood quietly, the water reaching up to his neck as I began to massage it. "If nothing else, at least you'll be clean," I told him as I continued to massage.

His scrawny little neck looked even more fragile with its wet hair plastered flat. He allowed all my ministrations without protest. I dried him with a soft terry cloth towel warmed up in a microwave oven. "It didn't work," I thought. "But I won't give up. I'll try it tomorrow, and the day after tomorrow! We'll lick it yet, Maxie!" And lick it, we did. Little by little I began to feel his neck losing its tightness, until one day Maxie barked shrilly as a mail truck drove to our door.

"We did it!" I cried triumphantly. "His voice is back!"

"You did it," George corrected. "Once again, you did it! You ought to advertise: 'care for hopeless cases'", he joked.

* * * *

For a while our life returned to its peaceful pattern. We enjoyed our large garden where the gardener and I had planted hundreds of daffodils and tulips. They produced a spectacular display of color in the spring, joined later by seventy five roses in my new rose garden. Ten gold fish that we bought the previous year, had survived the winter and were now splashing in the pond among the water lilies. Only now there were eighteen gold fish.

But trouble was brewing. George's health was rapidly deteriorating. His weakened heart soon undermined the function of his kidneys and the doctors prescribed a dialysis, a treatment that cleans blood of toxins. Three times a week George was now hooked-up to a machine that would "wash" his blood for three to four hours each time.

On the days of his treatment George was weak and disoriented, sometimes loosing his balance and falling down. As his illness worsened, the doctors recommended that he stay in bed for most of the day. He did not protest. While only a year ago he would've put up a fight against such suggestion, now he meekly agreed.

All our animals, three dogs and two cats, could hardly wait for him to get into his room. The little dogs and the cats would jump onto his bed even before he would be ready to get there himself.

I tried to protest, saying that it wasn't hygienic. "After all, they're animals, their feet are dirty, they shed their hair and they may even have fleas," but George ignored my objections.

"I like them around me," George would say petting one or another of the creatures cuddling next to him. Only Pepper remained off the bed, due to his size. But his head often rested on George's pillow as he would gaze at him with his soft intelligent eyes.

I gave up. I knew that the hygiene of George's environment was really not important anymore. He was sinking fast and his doctors had advised me not to deny him anything that might make him happy. "So, be it," I thought. "Let him have his animals."

George was especially fond of Feather. She was diagnosed as having diabetes and she craved attention. She was rapidly becoming blind. George identified with her increasing weakness and insisted on having Feather sleep in his room. He helped her climb up on his bed for soon she was too weak to manage it by herself. He watched that every piece of furniture in his room was put exactly at the same place so that the blind dog wouldn't bump into it.

Every morning now I gave her insulin shots and cooked a special diet of rice and chicken. But she was dying, I could see that.

One morning, while George was at the dialysis center hooked up to his machine, Feather died.

George was devastated. "I'll be the next," he predicted.

We buried Feather in the garden and planted some tulips over her grave.

* * * *

George stayed at the hospital three times that year. "I'm not giving up," he told his doctor. "I'll fight. I'm not ready to die. My inspiration is one of my own dogs, Max."

"A dog?"

"Yes. I'll send you a book about him. My wife wrote it. It tells all about his fight for his life. Max was a survivor. He's my hero."

Despite his resolve, George had lost his battle. He did not return home after his subsequent stay at the hospital.

* * * *

The most terrible months of my life followed. The animals shared my grief. Little Max, frightened by my frequent outbursts of sobbing stayed out of my way, watching me from under a chair. But Pepper never let me out of his sight. He followed me around as I aimlessly wandered from room to room, he stayed close to me as I tried to work in the garden. He rode with me in the car, jumping in the moment I would open the door and he slept next to my bed, something that he had never done before.

The cats, always independent, suddenly became clinging and talkative, greeting me with various tones of meowing and purring. They too, must have known that I needed affection.

My grief devastated me, but no matter how low I might have felt, the animals demanded attention. I had to take care of them. I had to feed them, clean after them, walk with them and play with them. And so, little by little, my acute feeling of loneliness began to subside, helped by the affection of my animals.

"Life must go on," I kept reminding myself, repeating one of George's favorite sayings. As time went by, I began to write again, to make plans for the future and even to laugh. My son, Ron, and his wife had a new baby whom they named after me. This baby, more than anything, gave a jump-start to my life.

I felt alive again. Life was going on.

Pepper's Ordeal

A new, frightening incident affecting one of my dogs, plunged me into a vortex of anxiety again. My gentle Pepper was stolen. Pepper was gone.

"Why me?" I cried in despair. "Why is it always my animals who are prone to tragic accidents? Am I cursed?"

It all started with a garden gate that a meter reader failed to close.

Pepper dashed out, vanishing in the hills surrounding the house. I wasn't home at the time and Pepper must've been gone for at least three hours by the time I returned.

I jumped back into the car and began canvassing the neighborhood, driving slowly up and down the hills, calling Pepper. To no avail.

Toward the night the hills around my house became shrouded in a thick fog. The canyons became invisible, the road leading to the house all but disappeared. One could hear the cars as they cautiously made their way up the hill, but one could not see them. The fog crept right to my deck creating the impression that the house was a ship, adrift on an endless calm ocean. Normally I would've enjoyed the sensation of being adrift, but not now, when I was worried sick about my lost dog. Can he find his way home in such total nothingness? Even if his acute sense of smell would lead him home, he could be killed on the road. No one could see him in this fog.

I hardly slept that night. I kept getting up and going into the garden with a flashlight, calling Pepper, hoping that he would be at the gate, waiting to be let in.

In the morning I placed an ad in the local paper describing the lost dog, offering a hundred dollar reward for the information about him. I made copies of Pepper's photo and distributed them among the neighbors' mailboxes.

My neighbors were sympathetic. They all liked Pepper. They promised to be on the lookout for him.

I checked with the animal shelter and with the highway patrol but there were no reports about a brown Doberman-dead or alive. Pepper had vanished.

* * * *

Pepper was bewildered. Only moments before he was loping over the hills, enjoying his illicit freedom but slowly becoming aware that he ought to head home. His stomach reminded him that it was eating time and that meant-home.

Instead, he was locked up in a tight, dirty cage, reeking of many dogs and their urine. The cage rattled in the back of a car, a strange, unfamiliar car that sped along the freeway. The person who drove the car was also unfamiliar. Actually, she was mean. She whipped him with a rope and his back and flank still smarted.

Pepper couldn't understand why he was in this car. He had been exploring the country, enjoying his adventure of running away, but the novelty of his freedom was wearing out when he encountered this stranger.

At first-she seemed to be friendly. She called him 'here, boy' and offered him a biscuit. He took the biscuit. He was hungry. He had no reason to mistrust her; people were always kind to him. He wagged his tail, asking for another biscuit. Instead, she grabbed him by his collar and pulled him toward her car.

Instinctively, Pepper knew that she was dangerous. He refused to follow her, but she held him tightly and as he struggled and twisted, she slipped a noose over his neck.

She was very strong and she lashed at him several times, hitting him hard across his back. Pepper had never been whipped and he howled in pain. She gripped the rope, allowing Pepper to exhaust himself by thrashing and jumping, tightening the noose around his neck even more as he tried to get away.

Two young boys helped the woman to shove Pepper into a cage and there he was, going somewhere with someone who smelled of evil.

Pepper was thirsty but there was no water. He remembered how his masters always kept a water dish whenever he accompanied them on an automobile trip. It felt so good to be able to lap fresh cool water whenever he wanted to! Pepper barked, to let the woman know that he was thirsty. She paid no attention. He barked again. "Shut up!" she shouted crossly.

Pepper was exhausted. It seemed to him that he was in that car forever. The wire cage was too small for him to lie down. If he knew how to tell time, he would've known that he was standing in that cage for almost two hours.

Finally they arrived at some unfamiliar place and the woman opened the cage. "Get out, you cur," she pulled him out by the rope. A loud chorus of growls and barks met them. The place was full of dogs, all looking mean, all locked up in rusty cages.

Pepper sat down on the dusty ground. "Get up!" The woman kicked him with her heavy boot and pulled on the rope. Choking, Pepper got up. The woman led him to a wooden shed. She took his blue collar off, glancing at his license and the name tags with the telephone number of his masters.

"Pepper, eh?" she sneered reading his name. "We'll see how 'peppery' you are!"

She tied him to a post and with her foot pushed a dish of dirty water toward him. He tried to drink, but the water could barely trickle into his parched throat squeezed tightly by the rope. The woman disappeared behind the sheds and Pepper heard the car engine start again. She was gone.

Pepper tried to lie down but the rope was too short. It cut painfully into his neck, squeezing his throat. He gave up trying to get out of the noose. He realized that the more he fought, the tighter it became. The ground under his feet was dirty and hard. It smelled of excrement but Pepper was too exhausted to care. He sniffed the air and he listened to the other dogs, trying to catch a friendly message, but there was none. What he had smelled, was danger. What he had heard in the dogs' howls and snarls, was hatred.

His instinct had told him that this hatred was aimed at him. He was in mortal danger.

.   .   .   .

I was becoming desperate. Whom could I call for help? What can I do to find my dog?

Help came from an unexpected source. Two boys, Tommy Owens and Bruce Lambert appeared at my gate about two days later. They claimed that inadvertently they helped a woman to kidnap my dog. They were paid five dollars to help her to get him into her car.

"Tell me, tell me, tell me all about it!" I cried. "Do you know who this woman is? Where did it happen? Tell me!"

The boys seemed to hesitate to give me more information.

"I'll give you your reward, don't worry," I said, thinking that they didn't want to say anything more unless they were paid.

"It's not that," said the dark-haired older boy named Bruce. "We just don't know where to start."

"Start from the beginning. Where did it happen and how can you be sure that it was my dog and not this woman's?"

"We're sure, " said the other boy, the be-freckled chubby Tommy. "We saw the dog's name on his tag-Pepper. He was a red Doberman and..."

"And he growled at the woman and tried to bite her. He didn't want to get into her car," Bruce joined, eager to talk now.

"That's when this woman asked us to help her to shove him into her station wagon. She had a rope around his neck...He was choking as he was fighting with her.. He had a blue collar on, just as you described in your ad, and we could see his name 'Pepper'."

"She kept hitting him with a rope and he yelped. She told us that he was the most disobedient dog that she ever had. "

"She called him ornery," Tommy added.

"Yeah. We helped her to get him into her car and she gave us five bucks."

"Where did it happen?"

"At the picnic grounds, near Toro park. We were there playing catch. Then we noticed this woman trying to get the dog into her car. She had a rope around his neck and he jumped and bucked like a bronco at a rodeo. We thought it was cool."

"Yeah. He didn't act as if he were her dog, " said Bruce. "He acted as if he hated her. We talked about it after she drove away. We thought that she must've been a mean person the way she treated this dog. She really hit him hard, several times. He yelled in pain."

"Then, when we saw your ad-we knew right away that he wasn't her dog. She was stealing him."

"And we helped her to steal him. But it wasn't our fault, honest. We didn't know that he wasn't her dog "

"I don't blame you, boys. In any other circumstances you should've been praised , if anything, for helping someone. Do you, by any chance, remember what kind of a car she was driving?"

"Yeah. It was a station wagon, all beat-up, really old, with wooden sides."

"It was dusty, too. Kind of muddy, like, she drove it on a country road."

"And it had several large wire cages inside. We pushed Pepper into one of them."

"She said that she lived on a ranch south of Salinas. She raised dogs."

"How old, would you say this woman was? How was she dressed?"

The boys looked perplexed. "I dunno", Tommy finally said. "She looked old. Not as old as you, but old. Maybe forty."

I suppressed a smile. Forty! Oh, to be forty again!

"Did you notice her license plate numbers by any chance?"

"Nope. But the plates were the old California plates, black background with yellow numbers, I remember that."

"Yes, they surely are the old California plates. There aren't many of them left," I said, thinking, "it may narrow the search for the car."

"She was wearing cut-off jeans and a T-shirt," Tommy added. "And cowboy boots."

"Well, that won't help us much. Everybody wears jeans and T-shirts now," I said.

"I would recognize her if I saw her again," Bruce said.

"Me, too," Tommy joined. "She looked weird. Her hair was cut short like a guy".

"And she had a humongous earring in one ear. Only one earring. It looked like a bunch of grapes but it was made of coins."

As I listened to the boys , a thought began to formulate in my mind. I would need help in tracking this woman down. The boys seemed to be fine, earnest kids, who were sincerely sorry that they had inadvertently helped to kidnap my dog. I would need them to identify the woman if I ever found her.

"I'll tell you what, boys. How about helping me track this woman down and try to rescue Pepper? I'll give you your reward. You've earned it. But if we find this woman and get Pepper back, I'll double the reward. How about it? Do you think you can help me?"

"Cool!" the boys exclaimed in one voice. "Sure, we'll help you!"

"My uncle is a cop. He's with a K-9 unit . You know, the cops who work with dogs as their partners. He will help us, I know," Bruce volunteered.

"Terrific! Tell your uncle exactly what has happened. Describe to him all your observations. Ask him what course of action must be taken to locate this woman. I suppose it will be difficult since we don't know her name or anything about her."

"But we do know that she's from somewhere south of Salinas and that she drives an old-fashioned station wagon with black license plates. And, we know that she raises dogs."

"These are good leads, I suppose. Police can find criminals with much less information," I said as I wrote two checks for fifty dollars each and handed them to the boys. "A policeman can do a lot with that information."

"Unless she lied," Tommy said darkly.

• • • •

In response to Bruce's telephone call, officer Bud Lambert arrived at my house during his lunch break. He was a pleasant young man of about thirty, with a shadow of a new mustache that he kept touching self-consciously as if to re-assure himself that it was still there. He readily agreed to help us.

"I'll do it on my own time. I'm a dog lover myself, so I know how you must feel."

"Thank you, Officer Lambert, I appreciate it."

"Call me Bud." He touched his mustache.

"Yes. Bud."

"Actually, I have a hunch that I may know something about this woman," he continued. "For some time now we have heard rumors that there is a dogfighting ring operating south of Salinas.

It is illegal, of course, to run dogfights and cockfights, but the operators are very clever. They constantly change their locations, sort of, like a floating crap game, if you know what I mean."

"How do they run these dogfights ?" I felt chill creep down my spine. Pepper, in a dogfight! The thought of it made me sick.

"Well, they use pit bulls. They train them to be especially vicious. The dogs usually fight to their deaths."

"But, Uncle Bud, Pepper is not a pit bull. He's a Doberman," Bruce said. "Why would they want him?"

"For training purposes. For training the pit bulls. The pit bulls are too valuable for them to risk an injury in training fights, so they use other breeds of large dogs, such as Dobermans and German Shepherds, who can put up a good fight. To them they are expendable."

"What does it mean?" Tommy asked.

"It means that the operators don't care if the target dogs get hurt or killed. They are expendable. As long as their own pit bulls are safe. A lot of money is made on dogfights. The operators are ruthless people, who don't give a damn about the dogs as long as they make money for them."

"My God! My gentle Pepper would have no chance against the pit bulls!" My eyes filled with tears.

"He wouldn't," Bud agreed. "The operators usually let loose several of their dogs against the target dog. Big money is involved in a real dogfight, so they train their pit bulls to be killers. They start by training their dogs to be vicious when they are still puppies. They use fishing poles with bait attached."

"Fishing poles?"

"Yes," he said. "It makes one sick just to think how cruel they are!"

"How do they do it?" Tommy asked.

"They make an enclosure where they put several young pit bull pups. Then, a man with a fishing pole would stand on the outside of the enclosure and wave the fishing pole over the pups. They would jump and try to snatch the bait off the pole."

"What would be the bait?" I asked.

"A cat."

"What?"

"A live cat, tied by the tail."

A cry of horror rose from my throat.

"Yes, a live cat! The pups would tear it to pieces as they jumped, fighting with each other for a better bite. As the pups grow and become more and more vicious, they would be introduced to a larger prey. Some medium - size dogs. Then, when the trainers decide that the pit bulls have learned how to be killers, they put them in the bigger arenas against some big dogs, like your Pepper, to keep them in fighting shape."

"Dear Lord! Can't anything be done about It? What about the SPCA? Can't the Society for Prevention Cruelty to Animals do something about it?"

"Sure. We were able to raid some of the dogfights, but still, they keep springing up here and there, like mushrooms. There is a whole chain of these illegal operations in many rural communities."

"Bud, if you know where it is, let's go there now! " I said wiping my eyes. "We can't waste a minute! They'll kill my Pepper for sure!"

"I can't go today, but I'll tell you what we'll do. Tomorrow I'm off duty, so we'll go tomorrow. Meanwhile," he raised his hand seeing that I was about to interrupt him, "meanwhile, you and the boys can drive through the neighborhood. Case the joint, so to speak. Take along your camera. Take pictures of every detail, all of the ins and outs of the property and so forth. You have a good start already. If my hunch is correct, just south of Salinas, near Solidad, you'll find a small arena where they hold these clandestine dogfights. I'm almost ninety per cent sure that the woman who stole your dog is a member of that dogfight ring. We had other reports about her. She even tried to 'adopt' four large dogs from the animal shelter. They might still have her car license numbers."

"Did they let her have the dogs?"

"No. They thought her application looked fishy. No one adopts four big dogs. One, or maybe even two big dogs, but four? They refused the adoption. However, they kept her application on file and notified us."

"Thank you, Bud. Are you with me, kids?"

"We sure are," said Bruce.

"If I'm right, you'll find this arena just a few miles before you reach the Pinnacles," Bud continued, as he drew a rough map.

"But be careful. The gangsters are a bunch of tough cookies. If the property is posted 'No Trespassing', don't go in."

"If we run into someone, we'll ask for the directions to the freeway. We'll say that we're lost," Bruce said.

Bud and I laughed. "You've thought of everything already," Bud said. "Good luck." He twitched the little growth over his lip again. "On the second thought...Don't go. It might be dangerous. We'll go together, tomorrow."

* * * *

"I am going there. Now," I said after Bud left.

"We'll come with you," the boys said. "We'll be careful... We'll just look around."

"OK. Let's go."

I drove south along freeway 101. "Watch for the turn-off to the Pinnacles," I said to the boys.

The Pinnacles was a craggy formation of huge rocks and caves, one of the natural wonders of California that was part of the National Parks system. Somewhere nearby we were to find a dirt road that would lead us to the secret arena.

As Bud had told us, this arena was originally used for staging cockfights. After the cockfights were raided by the authorities, the arena was abandoned. But not for long. The rumor was that it was enlarged and back in operation again, this time for dogfights.

"So far we haven't raided it," Bud had told us. "We don't have enough manpower to follow every rumor but if there is any evidence that there are fighting dogs there, we'll go in and close it down."

"What about the operators of the illegal enterprise ? Will you arrest them?"

"If we catch them. Most of the time they manage to escape. It's an international ring of illegal operations, spreading all the way to Mexico and beyond. The organizers escape across the border and wait until the heat is off. Then they return and start all over again, either with the cockfights or dogfights. As I said, there is a lot of money involved."

"I just hope it won't be too late for my Pepper," I thought as I drove along the freeway.

"The exit to the Pinnacles!" Tommy cried. The sign ahead informed us that the Pinnacles were still fifteen miles away. We exited the freeway and almost at once found ourselves on a narrow two-way road.

"OK boys, watch for the country lane. It should be on our right, about three and a half miles further on," I said consulting Bud's map.

I drove slowly, trying not to miss the lane. On both sides of the road there were vineyards planted in neat rows that seemed to cling to the rising hills. The road climbed up, toward the Pinnacles, the dark formation of stone that began to take shape in the distance as if it were a medieval city of impenetrable castles surrounded by crenelated walls.

Normally, I would've been eager to explore this fantastic phenomenon of nature, but not today. Today, I was thinking only of Pepper. Was he there, at that evil place where people paid money to see the dogs tear one another to pieces? Was he still alive or was he already sacrificed for the benefit of the inhumane monsters?

"The road! There it is!" Bruce pointed to the right.

We saw an unpaved country lane that looked as if it hadn't been driven upon for a long time. Tall weeds grew in the middle of it and even the wheel ruts sprouted grass.

"A good sign. It doesn't look like there has been much traffic on this road. Perhaps they haven't yet started their operations," I thought. "But of course, they still may have killed Pepper while training their monstrous dogs for the fights."

We drove along the bumpy lane for about a mile, seeing nothing but abandoned dried-up old orchards and tall dusty weeds. No buildings of any kind. No arena. Nothing.

"Are you sure that this is the right road?" Tommy asked. "Shouldn't we go back?"

"No. It's the first country lane on the right according to Bud's map. He said it would be difficult to find."

"There's an old fence.. And some shacks," Bruce said suddenly, pointing to a cluster of trees on his left.

"Where?"

"Behind the trees. There, look!"

I drove a few more yards and then, I too, saw a rusty chain-link fence and several dilapidated wooden shacks.

"OK, kids, this is it." My mouth went dry as I slowly drove toward the fence.

It was about four feet high and it was broken in many places, but its gate, blocking the road, was secured with a shiny new padlock. I could not drive any further.

"Is there any arena? I can't see," I asked the boys.

"I'll climb over the fence and take a look," Bruce suggested.

"No, no! Let me think..."

"There're no signs of No Trespassing," Tommy said. "We can sneak in."

"No. We don't know who might be there. The dogs might be around... Let me think," I said trying to bring to mind some course of action that I might have seen in some movie about a daring rescue. Nothing came to my mind.

"Turn your car around for a quick get away," Bruce suggested.

"Good thinking!" I backed up and turned the car around facing the road again. "Any other suggestions?"

"Yes. Sound the horn. If anyone is there, they'll come to the fence to investigate."

"Hey, you're terrific! A real detective! " I hit the horn several times. A cacophony of barks ensued.

"The dogs! They're there! This is the place ! " Tommy whispered, his face turning pale. Even his freckles seemed to lose their color.

We waited, expecting someone to emerge from behind the shacks. Perhaps, even the mysterious woman...

No one appeared at the fence.

"The dogs must be locked up," I said. I hit the horn again. Among the hysterical rasping barks I thought that I heard the familiar, deep-throated voice of my Pepper.

"He's there..." I whispered. "Pepper... He's there!" I sounded the horn several more times, in a pattern that was familiar to my dogs. I always used it to alert them of my arriving home. It usually stopped them from barking, telling them that it was I and not some stranger who was about to enter the property.

Now I wanted Pepper to do the opposite, to keep barking, to lead me to where he was. I concentrated on sending him a mental message" keep barking, boy, don't stop, keep barking!"

And he understood me. He kept barking, loud and clear.

"I am going in. Pepper is calling me," I said. "Watch the road. If anyone shows up, sound the horn, SOS. Do you know the signal?"

"Yes. Three short—three-long—three-short. SOS." Bruce was confident.

"Right. Stay in the car. Keep it locked and keep the engine running," I instructed, collecting Pepper's leash and a spare collar from the back seat. "Under no circumstances get out of the car. Sound the horn continuously, if needed, but don't get out of the car. This whole enterprise may become very dangerous. We may need to make a quick getaway. So, don't add to our problems by being caught out of the car, OK?"

"OK. But what if the dogs are on the loose?"

"They would've been here at the gate already. No, I think the dogs are locked up."

"Are you sure that it's Pepper's bark?" Bruce was obviously worried.

"I'm sure. I know his voice," I said.

"Shouldn't we come back tomorrow with Uncle Bud?" Bruce was reluctant to let me go.

"We're already here. Tomorrow may be too late. They may set their dogs on Pepper tonight," I said over my shoulder as I squeezed through the broken fence. "Just stay in the car!"

I felt suddenly calm. I wasn't aware of the dryness in my mouth nor the tremble in my legs. I went briskly toward the sheds and around them.

And, there it was. The arena.

It was the size of a small parking lot, no bigger than for three or four cars, surrounded on three sides by rough bleachers made of planks. On the fourth side the arena was blocked by a dozen of weather-beaten sheds, gray and rickety, some without doors or roofs. The sheds prevented the arena from being seen from the road. Through the gaping door frames of the sheds I could see several rusty cages, each containing a stocky dog. The pit bulls!

The dogs were in a frenzy, throwing themselves against the wire of their cages, trying to get at me. I prayed that the cages were securely locked. Even if only one dog got out, I had no chance.

At the last shed I saw Pepper. He wasn't in a cage, thank God! He had been tied down to a stout post with a rope that choked him each time he tried to free himself. The more he struggled, the

tighter the noose cut into his flesh. Seeing me he hurtled himself toward me, but the short rope cruelly held him prisoner. He coughed, choking, almost suffocating.

"I must calm him down before he kills himself," I thought. "Pepper, sit!" I called. He continued to struggle, jumping sideways, losing his balance, the rope holding him on his feet.

"Sit!" I ordered, trying to sound as if nothing was wrong.

He paused and stood panting rapidly.

"Stay," I ordered sternly, realizing that he could not "sit". The rope was too short. It held him up in a standing position. "Stay!" I repeated, hoping that he won't try to free himself before I was ready.

He obeyed. He stood, motionless now, breathing shallowly, waiting for me to help him. I slipped his collar over his neck and loosened the rope until I could remove it. He tried to lick my face, the stub of his tail wagging fast, but I had no time for his gratitude. "Let's go my friend, we're not out of the woods yet! Let's go!"

I started walking as fast as I could, cursing myself for not changing my shoes to sneakers before we left home. It wasn't easy to move over the uneven terrain, over ruts and debris of broken bottles and beer cans that cluttered the filthy yard. Pepper kept pulling, sensing the danger, eager to get out of that dreadful place.

The dogs in the cages went berserk. They snarled at one another, saliva dripping from their gaping mouths. They were confused as to whom they hated most-Pepper and me or each other. I felt their fury. It surrounded us like a poisonous cloud or was it their hot, stinking breaths that I smelled? I felt their urge to pounce on us, to tear us to pieces. "If they break out of their cages - we will be dead, for sure," I thought, starting to run.

Then - I heard the signal. SOS... and again, SOS... SOS...

Three short - three long - three short blasts of my car horn.

I ran faster, but my strength must've been all spent. I stumbled and fell, my right ankle badly twisted.

"Open the car door! " I yelled. "Call Pepper to get into the car!" I let go of his leash. "Go, Pepper! In the car!"

Confused, Pepper refused to go. "In the car, in the car!," I yelled at him pushing him toward the fence.

"In the car," the boys called, "in the car!"

The dog still couldn't understand why he had to go in the car without me. He heard the urgency in my voice. His training old him to obey but his tendency was to cling to me, rejoicing at our reunion.

"Get - in - the - car!" I yelled at him. This time he understood. I wanted him to obey. He would obey.

He ran toward the fence. The locked gate blocked his way. He hesitated and looked back at me. For a moment I thought that he was going to come back to me. I hobbled on my badly sprained foot toward the fence.

"Pepper, this way, Pepper!" the boys called." Pepper stopped. He remembered the boys. They helped that woman to shove him into her car. Yet there they were, in the car that he knew so well, the car that smelled familiar and safe. Pepper was now totally confused. He made several tentative steps toward the hole through which I came in.

I gave a sigh of relief. He found the way!

But he didn't see the hole. He was back at the locked gate.

"Jump, Pepper, jump!" I screamed. He heard the desperation in my voice. He looked at me again, and then, with one mighty jump, he rose over the fence.

"Good boy!" I shouted. I could see the boys flinging the car door open and Pepper getting in.

"Lock the car! " I yelled. "Keep Pepper out of sight!"

With Pepper safely in the car, I prepared myself for a confrontation with ... I didn't know what.

I heard the sound of the approaching car, but not from the direction of the road. In a moment, someone would confront me. "It was stupid not to check whether there was another entrance to this place," I thought.

The car, an old wood-sided station wagon came slowly to a stop. A husky woman in reflective sun glasses that looked like two round mirrors and made her eyes invisible, faced me through the open car window.

She looked tough. Her hair was cut very short and her ears protruded as if they were the handles of a French soup cup. Under one ear there dangled a long heavy earring of golden coins. It almost reached her shoulder.

"Who are you?" she demanded getting out of the car. She was wearing heavy boots and cut-off jeans along with a dirty T-shirt with a logo of the SPCA.

"SPCA ? Boy, that's a switch!" I thought.

Aloud, I exclaimed, trying to sound sincere, "Oh, I'm so glad to see you! I sprained my ankle climbing the rocks at the Pinnacles and I hoped that I could use your telephone to call my son for help. I'm with my grandchildren," I added, speaking fast, hoping that Pepper would keep quiet.

She stared at my swollen ankle and then at my shoes. "Only a fool would climb the rocks in those shoes!" she sneered.

"I know. It was crazy of me even to try," I laughed, trying to ingratiate myself "But you know, the kids... they wanted me to climb with them," I let it trail, as if I were a model grandmother, ready for any sacrifice for the sake of her grandchildren, but was too modest to say so.

"How come you didn't use the phone at the ranger station at the Pinnacles?" She looked at me with open hostility.

I had to think fast. "I should've. But at the time I thought I could make it home. But then, the foot began to swell and throb and I knew that I wouldn't be able to drive. So, I decided to call my son. This place was the first that we saw..."

"You couldn't have seen it from the road," she interrupted.

"I mean, we didn't see it, of course," I pretended to laugh, "we saw the road and we knew that it would lead us to a house or a ranch, where I could get to the phone. May I use your phone?" I asked sweetly, knowing that there was no phone and not even any human dwelling on the property.

"I ain't got no phone," the woman said curtly. "And I ain't buying your story, either."

"But look at my foot!" I started, and then thought better of it. Why should I try to play for her sympathy? All I wanted was to get out of there in one piece.

"I'm sorry," I said, hobbling toward the hole in the fence through which I came in.

The dogs in the cages choked on their fury. But I was out of their line of vision now. The woman yelled at them and they began to quiet down.

"The dogs from Hades... " I thought. "That's what they are, the dogs from Hell!" Almost safe, only yards from my car, I suddenly grew brave. I waved to the woman who was still watching me and shouted, "I see that you like dogs. Me too, there's nothing that I wouldn't do for my dogs!"

I heard the lock in my car click, indicating that the boys unlocked the door. "Bye-bye, now. Nice meeting you!"

I climbed into the idling car and gunned the engine. "Let's get out of here!'

"It was her! " Tommy exclaimed dramatically. "I recognized her right away!"

"Me, too," Bruce joined. "Even with her dark glasses."

"Yes, your description of her was perfect. Including the earring."

My ankle had swelled to a double of its size. It throbbed and it was torture to drive. I took my shoes off. Trying to distract myself from pain, I continued, "Yes, boys, you did everything just right. Including keeping Pepper quiet. I bet, she never even suspected that he was in the car."

"I hope she won't chase after us when she discovers that Pepper is gone," Tommy said looking nervously through the rear window.

The same thought had occurred to me also. I stepped on the gas.

"If a cop stops us for speeding, Bruce would have to bail us out," I said.

"How?" Tommy asked.

"By claiming his kinship to one of their fellow officers, his uncle Bud."

"Cool!"

"How's Pepper?" I asked. "He's awfully quiet."

"His neck is rubbed raw from the rope," said Bruce.

"It's all bloody," Tommy added.

"Poor Pepper. I was in such a hurry to get him out that I didn't even notice that he was injured. But we'll patch him up. He's free!" I shouted. Feeling that I was acting silly, I said, seriously this time, "I'm so grateful to you boys. It was your keen observations that led us to Pepper. And, perhaps even more. Perhaps, because of your information your uncle Bud will have enough evidence to raid this horrible place."

"We didn't take any pictures," Tommy said.

"Darn it! We should've taken along my camera!" I shook my head. "It totally skipped my mind. I was thinking only of getting Pepper out."

"Don't worry. Uncle Bud will do it tomorrow. He'll bring the police photographer," Bruce said.

I drove in agony. My sprained foot swelled to resemble a red cushion. I could hear Pepper panting behind the driver seat, but I couldn't see him. "He must be thirsty," I thought. "I didn't see any water at the shack."

Somehow, we arrived home without further complications. No one pursued us, no one stopped us for speeding. I hobbled to the house in my stockings, unable to put even my toes into the shoe. Pepper walked slowly ahead of me, holding his head down, his neck rubbed raw by the rope.

Maxie met us joyously, dancing around us, but Pepper did not respond to his greeting. He stood in the hall, with his head down. Maxie sniffed around him and probably detecting some hostile scents, retreated under his favorite chair. He watched us from there in silence, as if understanding the seriousness of the situation.

"It must be quite painful," I thought watching Pepper. "I'll need help cleaning his wound. Kids, will you help me?" I said aloud. "I can hardly stand up, but I need to clean Pepper's wound or it may get infected. Can you stay with me a little longer?"

"Sure. What do you want us to do?"

"First, call your parents and ask if you can stay here for a couple of hours."

"My Mom won't mind," Tommy said.

"And my parents are both at work. Nobody's home until late evening. We can stay here until dark."

"Just the same. Tommy, call your mother and tell her where you are. Ask her to pick you up here in a couple of hours, if she can. I don't think that I would be able to drive you home."

Tommy went to the phone.

"OK. Let's get going. First, get me some ice from the fridge and put it into a plastic bag. You'll find the bags in a box under the sink. I must get this swelling down. Second, we're all starving. There's some cold chicken in the fridge. And milk. Let's make some sand-wiches."

"I'm good at making sandwiches," Tommy boasted, coming back into the room, his freckled face looking as if it were sprinkled with cinnamon. "My Mom says she'll be glad to pick us up."

"Good. You make the sandwiches while Bruce and I attend to Pepper. I'll have to sit down, though. I must elevate my foot."

While Tommy was busy in the kitchen making sandwiches, Bruce helped me to settle down in an armchair in the living room. He piled up several small pillows on a coffee table and I placed my injured foot on them.

"Thanks. Now, on my desk in my bedroom is my checkbook. Bring it here. I want to give you guys your reward."

"You don't have to. We were glad to help you ."

"No, sir. A deal is a deal. Besides, you boys, really deserve your reward. I couldn't have saved my Pepper without you. So, let's get Pepper in and see what we can do for him," I said.

Pepper came to my chair on his own accord. He knew that we were going to help him. He stretched out at my feet, looking exhausted. I patted his head. "Poor boy, you went through hell!"

I instructed Bruce where to find the first aid items and together we began to clean the rope burns on Pepper's neck. He endured our ministrations with remarkable patience. He didn't fight us, nor did he try to escape.

I covered his neck thickly with a soothing antiseptic cream and wrapped it with a gauze bandage, but he didn't like it. Almost at once he began to scratch at it, trying to remove it. Afraid that he might hurt himself even more by scratching and infecting his would, I removed the bandage. Pepper relaxed and licked my hand.

"How's your foot?" Tommy entered the room carrying a tray with three plates of chicken sandwiches and three glasses of milk.

"It hurts. It throbs, too."

"Keep the ice pack on. That's what my dad does when some-one gets hurt."

"Is your dad a doctor?"

"No. He's a basketball coach at the high school."

We ate the sandwiches and drank our milk. Maxie crawled out from under the chair for a few bits of chicken, but Pepper refused to share our meal.

"Never mind. He'll eat when he feels better. His throat probably hurts as he tries to swallow. Poor dog, he went through such a traumatic time. I bet he knew that he would be killed."

"But how would he know?" Tommy asked.

"The pit bulls must've told him that they were going to kill him. They must've taunted him... They must've gloated over it."

The boys looked at me with incredulity. "How do you know?"

"I just know. Animals have a way of communicating their feelings to one another. The good feelings as well as the bad ones. Pepper knew, and he must've been terrified.."

Hearing his name Pepper lifted his head. His intelligent brown eyes stared at me with the intensity of deep love.

I kissed his forehead. "You're safe now, my dear friend."

* * * *

Next morning officer Bud Lambert and several other people from the police and animal regulations departments arrived at the hidden arena. Following our report, the authorities were ready to close down the illegal operation.

They didn't need to bother. When they arrived at the location they found nothing but the empty shacks. The pit bulls, the cages, everything was gone. And so was the woman with the long earring.

The author's three-year-old granddaughter and namesake, Kyra, and Pepper.